LIONS AND ACROBATS

poems by
Anatoly Naiman

translated from the Russian by
MARGO SHOHL ROSEN
& F.D. REEVE

ZEPHYR PRESS
Brookline, MA

Cover photograph © 2005 by Boris Trofimov
Book design by *typeslowly*
Printed by McNaughton & Gunn

Several of these poems appeared in *The American Poetry Review,*
The Harvard Review, and *The Mississippi Review.*

Zephyr Press acknowledges with gratitude the financial support
of Charles Merrill, the Massachusetts Cultural Council, and the
National Endowment for the Arts.

Library of Congress Control Number: 2005928828

09 08 07 06 05   8765432 FIRST EDITION

ZEPHYR PRESS
50 Kenwood Street
Brookline, MA 02446
www.zephyrpress.org

Table of Contents

In minutes of joy and hours of sadness, we feel and think in poetry: favorite lines come back to us, metaphors focus our attention; and when we turn to something Russian we find that Anatoly Naiman's strong, independent, subtle literary voice continues to flourish as it has flourished, published and unpublished, since Akhmatova dubbed the group of four around her—Dmitry Bobyshev, Joseph Brodsky, Anatoly Naiman and Evgeny Rein—her "enchanted choir." Unlike Brodsky and Bobyshev, Naiman has remained in Russia, where he continues to write poetry and prose. Although he has read and taught at universities in Europe, England and America, this bilingual collection is the first book-length translation of his poetry.

He is a poet of great intellectual dignity and power. In a day when the so-called "confessional poetry" that came in in the Fifties is fading and Language Poetry is forfeiting its claims and "New Formalism" seems to have nowhere to go, how astonishing to find an erudite poet in masterful control of his language and dedicated to poetry as an immediate expression of what is secret and mysterious about our lives, loves and dreams. He possesses the gift of sympathetically recording the essence of a simple relationship—a countryman plays with the idea of taking up with a countrywoman but she gets drunk—while simultaneously expressing the underlying, seemingly harmless, necessary mutual betrayals between them ("June Twelfth"). Exquisite is the cycle of poems (beginning with "Lullaby") about his granddaughter, Sophia, who, he fondly, patiently understands, will lose her spontaneity and special charm once she enters the social whirl of school. Of course, she wants to grow up—and she must. Of course, he doesn't want her to lose what he finds particular and precious—yet she must. Underlying the graceful poems and their sweet and obvious love is the poet's huge compassion for us, too, in our irrecoverable losses. Perception of the dichotomy makes the poems mini-dramas that seem drawn from our lives no less than from Sophia's.

Naiman was born in Leningrad in 1936. His mother Assya Averbukh grew up in Latvia, earned a medical degree at Montpellier and became a pediatrician. His father Henry, a technical engineer from Poland, was a follower of Tolstoy, and, as his son found out many years later, served time in prison for his faith. During World War II, or the Great Fatherland War as the Russians called it, Henry's plant—workers and families all—were evacuated to the Urals, so the four Naimans—Henry, Assya, and their sons Anatoly and Lev—escaped the "900 Days" blockade of Leningrad. In 1958, Naiman graduated from the Leningrad Technological Institute as a chemical engineer. During his years at the Institute he found his calling in poetry; because of censorship, half a lifetime passed before his work could be published.

Naiman came of age during the brief period of "The Thaw" when those who had survived the labor camps and exile were "rehabilitated" and artists, suppressed after the war, gained a few years of less onerous censorship. Poetry readings with the young, rising stars Yevtushenko and Voznesensky took place in Moscow's famed Polytechnicum; Ehrenburg and Dudintsev published challenging fiction; Tvardovsky edited *Novy mir,* which, in November 1962, published Solzhenitsyn's *One Day in the Life of Ivan Denisovich;* and Mr. Khrushchev welcomed Robert Frost. Two years later, Mr. K was gone and the gray "Period of Stagnation" had set in. It lasted for twenty-five years. Naiman greeted this period without protest and complaint. It was simply a fact of life that offered him a single natural response: a resistance that, while publicly undeclared, was complete and without compromises or concessions. In other words, internal emigration.

Naiman's intense and intelligent fascination with the world unerringly guided him to its essential core. In 1959 he learned by chance that Anna Akhmatova was living in Leningrad and spending her summers in Komarovo, a piney village suburb on the Gulf of Finland. He sought her out, drew Bobyshev, Brodsky and Rein along, and the four young poets discovered a world they had assumed to have been obliterated. Akhmatova became for them the "bridge between Not and Was in a wail of torments and rapture," as he writes in "Portrait of St. Petersburg after a Century," a living connection between their own generation and the exciting, innovative early decades of the twentieth century, the "Silver Age." The four young Leningrad poets became for Akhmatova the "Golden Cupola" of an era of poetry she helped shape. After her death, they became "Akhmatova's orphans." Now they are sometimes referred to as "the Leningrad school."

Throughout the sixties, seventies and eighties, Naiman's poetry was destined "for the drawer," and he was compelled to make his living as a translator. Leopardi's *Lyrics,* a collaboration with Akhmatova, came out in 1967; *Songs of the Troubadours* in 1979; *Flamenca* in 1983; *Floire and Blancheflor* in 1985; *Le Roman de Renart* in 1987; and *Le Roman des Sept Sages* in 1989, the year of incipient changes in the Soviet system and the year the first of his poetry collections was published in Russian but not in Russia—in the United States by Hermitage Publishing House. That year also saw publication of his fond biographical memoir of the friend whom he had served as literary secretary in the years before her death, *Stories about Anna Akhmatova* (published in English by Henry Holt in 1991 as *Remembering Anna Akhmatova*). Three years later, *Clouds,* a gorgeous folio of two poems in handwritten reproduction with English, French and Italian translations, and accompanied by artistic renderings, came out in Italy, and a book of stories in Russian, *The Statue of the Commander,* in London. In the last half dozen years, five novels and novellas have appeared in Moscow—from *B.B. et al.* to *Love Interest* and *A Disagreeable Man,* last year's *Each and Every,* and this year's *Kablukov.* His book about Isaiah Berlin, *Sir,* based on many long conversations between them, the publisher calls "not a biography, not a portrait, not a memoir [but] a novel about the epoch's need for such a man." In 1993, Hermitage published Naiman's second collection of poems in his native language, *Clouds at the Century's End.* Seven years later, *The Rhythm of the Hand* came out in Moscow; *Sofiya* in 2002; *Lions and Acrobats* in 2002. Forthcoming is his latest book of poems, *Extraterritoriality.* Naiman has won numerous awards, has been a Fellow at Oxford and at the Kennan Institute, and is a perennial candidate for Russia's Smirnoff-Booker Prize.

Although not published in book form until he was past fifty, Naiman remained patiently, perseveringly optimistic about literature's cultural role. As Brodsky noted in his afterword to Naiman's first published poetry collection, "this is a poet who was formed early, but incontrovertibly, who is especially gifted formally and whose technique is extraordinary, and who has never in the least betrayed his own personal idiom.... The tone of his poetry is above all meditative and elegiac, distancing itself from high pathos and often tinged with sardonic irony. He avoids the large forms and his main genre is the lyric poem, in which he is more often auto-biographical than narrative."

Except for two, the poems in this translated collection are selected from Naiman's latest volumes, and the two exceptions—"The less there is remaining to be known ..." and "A Wake for the Century"—are so recent that they anticipate the Russian publication of his forthcoming *Extraterritoriality*. The "Sophia" cycle is from a series of poems written as he watched his granddaughter grow. The remainder—indeed, the whole selection—is intended to give the English-speaking reader a mind-opening sense of the wonderful, wide range of rhythm, mood and experience that is Naiman's poetry. It leaps from celebration of alphabet sounds ("An ABC") to moving tributes, such as that to Isaiah Berlin ("On the Death of ***"), to an intellectually rigorous and humane view of our cultural tradition that folds inherited classical values into every moment of present experience as it shapes the future ("Along an Ancient Thought-Tree"). The self clothes itself, layer by layer, with the world ("I dress my heart ... "), and the eye that picks out what Blok called "the delicate flowers" of creative work—the "eyelash butterflies,... and flocks of strings and flutes, and lilacs breathing out [that] 'don't lie,'" ("Those eyelash butterflies ...")—conjures up a vulnerable, living, palpable world. As Naiman says point-blank in "The less there is remaining to be known ...," "it only makes a handful, but a handful holding all."

The translations don't represent a collaborative effort on each poem but a gathering of fifty poems each translated either by Margo Shohl Rosen, long a supporter of Anatoly Naiman's work and a close family friend, or by F. D. Reeve, for years an admirer of the poetry and now a warm acquaintance. Neither translator sets much store by theory, knowing that theories of translation have remained unsurprisingly constant over the millennia; often they seem to offer not much more than weak direction for reading actual samples. "Invisibility" is the standard by which all translations are generally judged, so the translator seeks to identify with the original, foreign author and to disappear in the work. "This is the most mischievous and comprehensive innovation," Doctor Johnson complained in the preface to his *Dictionary*; "if an academy should be established for the cultivation of our stile ... let them ... stop the licence of translatours, whose idleness and ignorance, if it be suffered to proceed, will reduce us to babble a dialect of France."

So, rather than belabor a theoretical approach, we turn, at publisher's request, to a discussion of the two "Lullabies," which "does seem ironic to me," Rosen noted in a letter to Reeve, "because it is the rare instance in which I took frightful poetic liberties and likewise the rare instance in which you chose the most strict obedience. Typically you are free where I am conservative, but it doesn't much matter to me which poems we look at as each, I've found, makes its own extremely idiosyncratic demands."

On the left, below, is the version included in the book. Both translators sought as much as possible to preserve the imagery and rhythmic pattern of the original, to add nothing, to keep their own voices out and to let Naiman's shine through.

Lullaby for Sophie

Fish is sleeping, floating on his fin,	The fly's asleep up on the ceiling,
Fly is sleeping, sticking to the ceiling,	the fish is sleeping on its fin,
Bird is snoozing, head beneath her wing,	the bird's head's underneath its wing,
Rover's chasing rabbits in his dream.	the dog is underneath my desk.
Star is sleeping high up in the sky,	The star is sleeping in the sky,
crowds are sleeping as they hurry by,	the crowd of people is rushing by,
train is sleeping—don't you think	the train's choo-chooing fast cross country,
it's funny?	
bumble-bee is dozing in his honey.	the bee's asleep in its own honey.
Sheep and she-wolf have to sleep apart—	The sheep and wolf sleep far apart—
sleeping both together wasn't smart,	they tried but couldn't sleep together—
winter's sleeping wrapped up all in white,	the winter sleeps in its white weather,
all the earth lies snug in bed tonight.	the round earth's tucked in its feather-bed.

Everyone is nodding off to sleep, John Donne in his pulpit counting sheep, church-bells in their towers sleep, John Donne, go ahead and sleep, your side has won.	The whole world's headed off to sleep, sleeping in his chair—John Donne; all the church bells soundly sleep; sleep, John Donne, your side has won.
Rest, Vladimir Solov'yov, your head, words of wisdom be your feather bed, let your thoughts be, it's no use to keep wasting them on Sophie, let her sleep.	Sleep, Vladimir Solovyov, beneath your quilt of words of wisdom, don't touch them more, don't expend them on Sofya now, let her sleep.
Sleep, Sophia—Sophie, go to sleep. First, though, go and brush your teeth and pee, lie down in the warmth of your cocoon, like the frog and hamster and raccoon.	Sleep, Sofya. Sonya, sleep. Before you do, go make peepee, come back, lie down in warmth and softnes the way a frog does or a hamster.
Sleepy breaths float up to God in heaven, try to count now all the way to seven, sleepy like a mouse, like grass and snow hush-a-bye. And off to sleep you go.	God can hear your sleepy sigh; now slowly count out one, two, three; like snow, like grass, like a mouse that creep so softly—shh. And you're asleep.

How delighted we translators would be if by the act of translating we could overcome all our native limitations. By reading and by assiduous attention to the terms and conditions of the original we can push our ignorance back a little. Certainly, by enjoying the privilege of working with a brilliant, renowned, living poet we can avoid inexcusable misinterpretations and false readings. Aware that every language has its own system of associations between symbols and referents, that no two languages are congruent, Naiman himself wants the body that is the poem to live freely in the regalia of its translation. He knows that even onomatopoetic forms are culturally conditioned: the American rooster crows *cock-a-doodle-doo* and the Russian cries *coo-ca-rieh-coó*.

Although the original is here on facing pages, we have gladly taken up the suggestion of laying some of our work down side by side with itself to show what necessarily happens in the move from one culture to another. In fact, we have selected the next example to show how the two of us—each holding to one general theory of translation—inevitably varies from poem to poem. Again, the published version is on the left:

A Toast

I drink to you, too.
　　—Anna Akhmatova

I drink to the land I love, but not
to what in it I've loved,
not to the lupine fading away
in the distance, as in Monet—
in general, not to a distant landscape
or one through a window or close
　　　　　　to my heart—
a view of the land has too much truth
　　　　　to escape
becoming a mere cliché.

Especially now that little is left
of what I loved before.
I drink to the land I love—to the light
that made loving it true;
to the ray, the stream of particles,
to the eyeless force by which it taught
the eyes to see and keep seeing
and started, land, by seeing you.

But above all, to the air filled
through and through with it,
the air with which I breathed the smoke
of the Fatherland borne
down on local woods and streams,

on snowfields and a flock of birds,
as a motionless face is fitted
with a still hot plaster mold.

To the invisible bread of the air—
to the draft out winter's window—
the air I gulp down,
chew over and over in my hungry mouth,
breathe in and out, burbling,
gurgling—to you,
steep slope of this nobody's earth,
place I've long called my own.

And I drink to you.
　　—Anna Akhmatova

I drink to my dear land—but not
to what I loved in it,
not to the lupines, yellowing,
far off, as in Monet;
And not at all to some far view
through glass, or in one's soul,

a landscape holds too many truths

to escape cliché.

What's more, there's almost nothing left
of what I loved. I drink
to my dear land—and to the light
in which its dearness grew,
that gleam, that flow of corpuscles,
the dazzling way it made
my eyes see everything, beginning,
my dear land, with you.

But, mainly, I drink to the air
that permeated through,
with which my fate was to inhale
my homeland's smoky pall,
which pressed against the streams
　　　　　　and groves

and snows and flocks of birds,
as if against an unmoved face
a still-hot plaster mold.

That stream unseen, that bread of air—
a casement window lets
it in—I eat it with my larynx,
my mouth chews hungrily,
by breathing which, by gurgling it,
by which I make a sound—
and called you, bed of earth,
I called you dear.

[XV]

We who offer you this book will be deeply pleased if the details of your admiration of Naiman's skill and courageous outspokenness lead you to affirm his generosity. His mind is as strong and iconoclastic as the best, but the distinguishing mark of his poetry is the relentless clarity with which he celebrates the finest, noblest, most fundamentally revolutionary and individual moments of our common culture. In his new novel, *Kablukov,* he has the scenarist Kablukov attribute capaciousness of spirit to his acquaintance Joseph Brodsky, "whom he met somewhere in Leningrad around 1960" and who had the habit of repeating everywhere and to everyone as an aphorism "The main thing is grandeur of design." After the umpteenth time, however, Kablukov says to him, "Enough. You can drop it. I've heard it, and for the others there's no point." Brodsky is dumb-founded, years later says he always considered Kablukov a spoilsport, a basketball player who couldn't do anything but "dump it in the basket." Brodsky is expansive, but doesn't like to be criticized. Kablukov is patient, observant, mildly cynical. Naiman has given Brodsky a tag that drives Kablukov to say, in effect, "lift the needle." In short, our magnanimous author hides behind his own protagonist to invest a remembered friend with "grandeur of design"—the attribute that most clearly defines himself.

January 2005

MARGO SHOHL ROSEN translated the following poems in this collection: *Along an Ancient Thought-Tree, Alone on a Hill, Water of the Neva and Hudson, Ode on an Easel, Voice of America, Gianni, Here an Attack of Lumbago, Worm, Portrait of St. Petersburg After a Century, May 9, An Empty Shop Window, The Pads of Your Fingers, Early Berry-Picking, In the Best Part of His Soul, From Prescriptions for Sleep, I Knew a Quartet of Poets, A Little Song, On the Death of ***, These Eyelash Butterflies, You Can, If You Like, Sing Two Figures, Lullaby for Sophie, What Can be Said, Fuga et Vita, Saturday's Dawning, Don't Brush Away That Butterfly, Whoever Has Gazed at the Night,* and *The Less There Is.*

A poet and translator, she was formerly assistant principal violist of the Anchorage Symphony Orchestra. Her work has appeared in the *London Review of Books, the Mississippi Review,* and *Oktyabr'.* At present she is a doctoral candidate in Slavic at Columbia University where she has written on Dante's influence on Akhmatova.

F. D. REEVE translated the following: *A Toast, Parable of the Elder Son, I Pull On Over My Heart, Eros, To an Infant, Sophie Is Eighteen Months, Sophie Is Two and a Half, Sophie Is Three and a Half, Sophie Is Four and a Half, Sonnet, Sophie Is Six, Sophie Is Seven, Sophie Has Started School, The Ballad of the Black Card, Crater, Circus, The Black-Winged Kite, You're Alone, Moods, An ABC, June Twelfth,* and *A Wake for the Century.*

Poet, novelist, critic and translator, he is professor of letters emeritus at Wesleyan University. He is the author of two dozen books (including *Robert Frost in Russia,* available in a new edition from Zephyr Press) of which the most recent are *The Return of the Blue Cat,* poems with a CD of his reading to the improvisational jazz of the trio Exit 59, and the novel *My Sister Life,* both published by Other Press.

for Svetlana Harris

По мыслену древу

Исайе

Как луч по стволу, как жар сквозь золу, как пар
от губ, на бегу к другим обратившихся с речью,
так мысль о коре, толпе и костре—в театр
вещей ускользнет, чтоб встать в реквизит вещью.

Взлетев на ольху, металась вверху мысль
о том, что внизу держу на весу я хворост
и слов нерасслышанных тот постигаю смысл,
что мысль россомахой была и есть, а ветвь—образ.

Снеси за кулисы всё до последних лепт,
всё, что имел, всё, чем себя измучил.
Я слов не слыхал, но долго махал вслед—
и вот их судьба: театр вещей, а не чучел.

Ведь в выдохе кроется голоса нервный пуск,
и звука его слушателю не сбавить:
становится сценой то, что для нас звук,
и увертюрой то, что для нас память.

Along an Ancient Thought-Tree

to Isaiah

As light stripes a tree-trunk, heat streams through ashes, steam puffs
from lips on its trip to others, attended by phrases,
so a thought about bark, a crowd and a bonfire slips off
to serve as a prop in the Theater of Shades.

Flying to an alder, scrambling up, the thought is
about how below I've balanced a load of brush
and am grasping the meaning of un-caught words:
that thought was and is a wolverine, and its form—the branch.

Sweep everything back-stage, to your very last mite,
all that you had, all you found so exhausting.
I didn't hear the words but waved as I followed their flight,
and their fate was this: the Theater of Things, not of straw men.

The nervous ignition of speech, after all, is breath,
its sound can't be lessened, once in the listener's ear:
what was for us a sound will become the stage,
and what for us is memory—the overture.

Тост

И за тебя я пью.
Анна Ахматова

Я пью за милый край—но не
за то, что в нем любил,
не за вдали, как у Моне,
желтеющий люпин,—
и, вообще, не за ландшафт
вдали, в окне, в душе—
в ландшафте слишком много правд,
чтобы не стать клише.

Тем более, почти уж нет
того, что я любил.
Я пью за милый край—за свет,
в котором стал он мил,
за луч, поток корпускул, за
то, почему, слепя,
всё видеть он учил глаза
и начал, край, с тебя.

Но, главное, за воздух, им
пронизанный насквозь,
за тот, вдохнуть с которым дым
Отечества пришлось,
припавший к рекам и леску,
снегам и стае птиц,
как к неподвижному лицу
еще горячий гипс.

За воздуха незримый хлеб—
из форточки струю—
который я гортанью ем,
голодным ртом жую,
дыша которым, клокоча,
звуча,—тебя, увал
земли, которая ничья,
я милым называл.

4

A Toast

I drink to you, too.
Anna Akhmatova

I drink to the land I love, but not
to what in it I've loved,
not to the lupine fading away
in the distance, as in Monet—
in general, not to a distant landscape
or one through a window or close to my heart—
a view of the land has too much truth to escape
becoming a mere cliché.

Especially now that little is left
of what I loved before.
I drink to the land I love—to the light
that made loving it true;
to the ray, the stream of particles,
to the eyeless force by which it taught
the eyes to see and keep seeing
and started, land, by seeing you.

But above all, to the air filled
through and through with it,
the air with which I breathed the smoke
of the Fatherland borne
down on local woods and streams,
on snowfields and a flock of birds,
as a motionless face is fitted
with a still hot plaster mold.

To the invisible bread of the air—
to the draft out winter's window—
the air I gulp down,
chew over and over in my hungry mouth,
breathe in and out, burbling,
gurgling—to you,
steep slope of this nobody's earth,
place I've long called my own.

Одинокое на холме

(Что такое дерево?—Дыры и пещеры,
как фонтанчик пляшущая в пустоте мошка,
скрипача, спеленатого в кокон, как торреро,
пассы, швы, вероники, петельки смычка.

А поскольку хочется больше, чем отмерено,
вот мы и отправились в счет грядущих лет:
Иванов в Италию—поглядеть на дерево,
Кириллов в Америку—тот увидеть свет.)

Вяза облетающего легкий шар и парус,
набранное золотом по контуру крыло
в голубое лоно, в ребра упиралось,
пчелками, чешуйками прядало, трясло.

Дерево горячечное обривали наголо,
а оно все тыкалось в мамку головой—
так они и ластились, два огромных ангела,
золотой—став бабочкой, ветром—голубой.

Но нужней и проще что-то было третье,
то ли, что спустился и не поднялся
этот блеск октябрьский в двух шагах от смерти,
то ли глаз, заметивший вяз и небеса.

Alone on a Hill

(What's a tree made of? Holes and deep recesses,
like a swarming spring of midges hovering in space,
a violinist's bowed designs, figure 8's and passes,
the fiddler like a matador cocooned in swathes of cape.

And since we always want a little more than we're allotted,
naturally we start into the years that lie in store,
Ivanov goes to Italy, to see a tree and draw it,
Kirillov to America—to meet the final shore.)

An airy globe, a sail of elm, leaves descending gently,
a wing with contours worked in gold, it leaned against the ribs,
against the light blue lap of sky, and leaning there it trembled
like a swarm of bees, a flash of scales, it shook and twitched.

And caught a fever, so they shaved it bare, but all the same
it kept on bumping up its head against its mama's sides—
gently they caressed each other, two enormous angels,
the blue—a wind, the golden one—a flock of butterflies.

Some third thing was also there, simpler and essential,
perhaps that the October light, two steps from death, didn't rise
once it made its bright descent, or it might have been
the eye that caught and noted there the elm against the skies.

Вода Невы и Гудзона

Дмитрию Бобышеву

Как странно: полжизни ходить по мостам над рекой,
пустой, ледяной, одинокой, пышной, угрюмой,
полжизни—нигде, и полгода в конце—над другой,
бегущей навстречу, бьющей копытцами в трюмы.

Ту первую взнуздывал камень по имени Петр,
по шкуре ее адамант проходился и грифель,
и сивка никак насечек и клейм не сотрет,
хотя и трясет три столетья, мятежная, гривой.

А эта, как после дистанции, в легком поту,
как после работы, в овес золотой океана
уходит пастись, как две капли похожа на ту—
весь мир охлестнула, что ли, она? Странно.

А город, по сути, что здесь, что тогда—Амстердам:
тот петрографический, камнем расчирканный короб,
в который суда волокут груз, вода—хлам,—
над вечной рекой ждущий конца город.

… Дается полгода прожить, как полжизни жил,
когда тебе душу вытесывал камень-диктатор,—
чтоб оттого смутиться, что мир не лжив,
и услыхать, как жизнь защелкивает замок метафор.

Water of the Neva and Hudson

to Dmitry Bobyshev

How strange: to walk half your life over bridges spanning a river,
empty, magnificent, icy, alone, morose it appears,
half a lifetime you're nowhere, and then at the end—a half-year
over another, galloping toward you, hooves pounding the piers.

Peter, a stone, was the one who reined in the first,
strewing slate and adamant layers from shoulder to flank,
and the gray won't ever shake off her brands and inlay,
although for three centuries now she's been tossing her mane.

But this one, as after running a distance, lightly perspiring,
as after a hard day of work, she heads out to range
in the oats of a golden ocean, is as like as two drops to the first one—
has she whipped round the width of the world? How strange.

In fact the city—both this one and that—could be Amsterdam:
petrographic, a basket battered and beaten by stone,
where ships haul in loads of cargo, and water hauls garbage and scum—
above the eternal river, the city awaiting its end.

… It's given to live half a year as you lived half a lifetime,
when your soul was being squared off by a dictator-rock,—
so that now your confusion can grow at the world not lying,
as you just catch the sound of life latching metaphor's lock.

Станковая ода

Д. С.

Безденежно и безнадежно,
чуть-чуть жеманно, в меру нежно
артист оглядывал модель,
то кистью пробовал, то тростью,
и каждый раз пугалась гостья,
в себе искусства видя цель.

Бежали дни, менялись стили,
со сцен натурщицы сходили,
потом художеств падишах
и маг, дарами мир осыпав,
с одним из двух сливался типов,
затвердевавших в витражах.

Номер один, живя в Нью-Йорке
или Париже, на конфорке
варил куриный суп с лапшой,
дитя-художник из местечка,
которого в санях овечка
везла к Медведице Большой.

А номер два, калиф Пальмиры,
крылами осенив полмира
подобно чудо-соловью,
искал гармонии в Париже
и откровений в чернокнижье
со ссылкой на "Нью-Йорк ревью".

....

Ode on an Easel

to D.S.

Without a hope, without a penny,
a bit affectedly, but gently,
the artist looked his model over.
He tried a brush, a charcoal stick,—
and every time his guest took fright
at seeing in herself art's object.

The days flew by, new styles were tried,
the models moved off to the side,
a newer kind of art was cast:
a sultan-wizard poured his gifts
into the world, from which were formed
two types, which cooled into stained glass.

The first type, living in New York
or Paris, simmered chicken soup
with noodles on a lone gas burner.
Born in a shtetl, this artist-boy
got carried via lamb-pulled sleigh
as far as the Great Bear.

The second type sought harmony
in Paris, read books of sorcery,
Palmira's Caliph he, whose view
spanned half the earth, as if he flew,
wings darkening the world below,
while quoting the *New York Review*.

....

В стекло пятнадцатого века
на дернувшую шкурой реку
перед прыжком в последний век
из бальных залов мы глазеем
монастыря, что стал музеем
земных молитв и звездных рек.

Река времен, в своем стремленье
бурля, становится нетленней
средь мира, не средь пустоты,
несет вчерашние газеты,
в которых вздувшиеся зеты
твердят, что с вечностью на ты.

В ней зыбью прыгает минута,
в ней есть энергия закута,
животный дух кровей и чувств,
которых теплоту и косность,
как время, производит космос
домашним способом искусств.

… Through five hundred year-old glass,
(before we leap into the next
one hundred years) we can discern,
past views of wrinkled river skin,
from ballroom halls we stand within,
a monastery, turned museum
of earthly prayers and starry streams.

Time's river, roiling in its urge,
becomes increasingly unspoiling
amidst the world, not emptiness,
and carries yesterday's top stories,
where bloated "X-es" still insist
Eternity and they are friends.

A minute capers in each ripple,
its energy—a barnyard sort:
that brutish breath of blood and senses,
whose warmth and sluggishness the cosmos
produces, making time as well,
by that domestic means, the arts.

Голос Америки

Роману

"На площади Мэдисон в сквере играет джаз".
Славно сказано, складно, как кукареку.
Губы щекочет звук и дрожит у глаз—
а почему б и не спеть, и не всплакнуть человеку!

Когда тебе 9 лет, из них 4 война,
и вдруг она кончилась, и переходят поминки
по-быстрому в танцы, шкатулка заведена,
и, черным маслом лоснясь, качается бок пластинки,

фанфара рыдает холодно и горячо,
шеллак поблескивает на скорости 78,
и сквозь него словно мерцает плечо,
мускусное, чернотой, уходящей в просинь.

Потом тебе 19: колониальных вакс
аромат источает другая шкатулка; надраен
хром радиоламп; саксофон называется сакс;
и как внушителен диктор под треск с мировых окраин!

Голос Америки, гудя, улетает во тьму:
там, на Мэдисон Сквер, то-то раздолье!
Там—и в Карнеги Холл. И какое кому
дело, кто этот Мэдисон—Джеймс или Долли?

Тромбон рыдает; футляр лежит на земле,
полный дождя и листвы; белки, налитые
восторгом, мерцают. И я хочу быть в числе
черных святых, когда в рай марширует святые.

На площади Мэдисон в сквере играет джаз.
Это—конец, и начало, и всё. Ничего не прибавишь
к этому—даже всхлипыванья каждый раз,
когда лиловый вибрафонист касается клавиш.

Voice of America

To Roman

"At Madison Square, in the park, jazz is playing."
Splendid, smooth words, like "cock-a-doodle-doo."
The sound tickles my lips and trembles in my eyes—
so why not sing out and shed a tear or two?!

When you're 9 years old, and 4 of those were war—
and suddenly it's over, and the wakes pass on
into lively dances, the record player's cranked up
and, shiny with oil, the record sways along,

a fanfare sobs hot and cold, the shellac
glistens at 78 rotations per minute,
and through it, somehow, a shimmying shoulder,
musky, showing black with blue-ish in it.

And then you're 19: a whiff of colonial wax
comes from another box; the chrome of the radio receiver
is all shined up; the saxophone is called a sax;
and the host, backed up by world-wide static, makes you a believer!

The Voice of America, buzzing, flies into the gloom:
right there, in Madison Square—liberty's strains!
And Carnegie Hall is there too. And who cares
which Madison it is—Dolly or James?

The trombone wails; its case lies on the ground,
full of green leaves and rain; whites of eyes gleam in
ecstasy. And I want to be in that number
of black saints, when the saints go marching in.

"At Madison Square, in the park, jazz is playing."
It's the end, and the start, it's all of a piece,
there's nothing to add—not even the sobbing
each time the lilac vibraphone player touches the keys.

Джанни

Змейка чернил на бумаге "манилла"
цвет изменила, смысл изменила
сразу со здравствуй на неразбър—
слух о писавшем приплелся с повинной,
время метнулось спиной буйволинной:
дней не осталось замуслить до дыр.

… Он появлялся в Крещенский сочельник,
теплый, как булка, белый, как мельник,
козьи сыры привозил и вино.
Жизнь осолив и культуру осалив,
чувствовал книгу профанную "Алеф"
только как речь он, а речь как кино.

Взмыв на Шри-Ланке, летел аэробус
с ним в Новый Год к Эвересту—он глобус,
словно квартиру, ключом отпирал:
в Лондоне спальня, прислуги каморка
в Вене, в Париже кухня, в Нью-Йорке
лифт, и брандмауэром—Урал.

Он полюбил нас—а что это значит:
лица без жалости, землю без качеств,
правда, язык наш—звездная ночь,
правда, что "здравствуйте"—то катастрофа,
правда, не Азия и не Европа,
спичка—для вписок, для вымарок—нож.

В Предсибирии, в Зауралии
из реки Сысерть
убежала Смерть,
прибежала в Рим
полюбиться с ним—
как-то слаще оно в Италии.

Gianni

The thin ink snake on manila paper
has altered its sense, altered its color,
all in a stroke, from "Hello" to "*illeg.*"—
the rumor has grudgingly turned itself in,
time jerked like the hide on a buffalo's spine:
no days remain to thumb through his pages.

… On Epiphany Eve he appeared at the door,
warm, like a bun, white, like a miller,
an armful of gifts, red wine and *chevre*.
He salted life, and sifted through culture,
the profane book "Aleph" for him was just speech,
and speech for him was the movies.

Then off to Sri Lanka, where an aerobus flew him
to Everest for the New Year—he unlocked the globe
as he would his apartment:
the bedroom in London, the maid's room
Vienna, in Paris the kitchen, in New York
the lift, the Urals his firewall.

He got to like us—and all that implies:
pitiless faces, land without qualities …
true, our tongue is a night full of stars,
true, our "Hello" is an all-out disaster,
true, it's not Europe, nor is it Asia,
a match is your pen and a knife your eraser.

> In Near Siberia, behind the Urals
> from a river's berth
> rose the specter, Death,
> ran off to Rome
> found him at home—
> it's sweeter, somehow, in Italy.

17

Это не "вечная память", а проба—
помнишь как, помнишь как, помнишь как … Что бы
вспомнить, с тобой о тебе говоря?—
милого Звево забавное слово;
с рейнским сухим судака разварного;
честность очков под ногами ворья.

Джанни (и колокол: джанни! джованни!),
ни отпеванье, ни расставанье—
чем встретить день студеный такой?
Кто из живых знает смерти меру?
Вставлю, пожалуй, в кассетник Карреру,
мессу креольскую за упокой.

> *Господь, прилей кровь моей вере!*
> *Господь, пожалей меня зверя!*
> *Господь, утешения двери*
> *открой скулящему псу!*
> *Господь, Отец мой небесный,*
> *твой дух и состав телесный*
> *внеси в закуток мой тесный,*
> *а я свою боль внесу.*

This isn't "rest in peace," it's rehearsal—
do you remember, do you remember … What
to recall, talking with you, about you?—
Svevo's witty repartee;
a dish of perch with dry Rhine wine;
the honesty of a pair of specs
under the boot of a thief.

Gianni (and bells tolling: gianni! giovanni!)
not a mass, not a parting—
how to face such a bitter cold day?
Who of the living knows death in its measure?
I'll play, if you like, a cassette of Carreras,
a Creole mass for the dead.

My God, put blood into my belief!
My God, be merciful to a beast!
My God, let consolation relieve
this whimpering cur's refrain!
My God, my heavenly Father,
bring your spirit and corporal matter
into this, my close, dark corner,
and I'll bring in my pain.

* * *

То—прострел в поясницу, то—неделю мигрень,
в марте—гастрит, в апреле—стенокардия,
про зубы или про грипп и рассказывать лень,
всю жизнь одно за одним, такая картина.

И что любопытно, хворь прыгает вверх и вниз,
одно идет за другим, но никогда не вместе—
это, как будет, показывает организм,
когда навалится разом всё, стало быть, к смерти.

Что это? сердце? ты тикало, как часы,
прощай! Мозги, в вас мир клокотал, как в воронке!
Желудок—знаток натюрмортов в каплях росы!
Прощайте, ветров ущелья и флейты—бронхи!

А жаль, так верно друг другу служили вы,
рудами и родниками кормясь своими,
так ткань была совершенна, так тонки швы,
что даже носили когда-то душу и имя.

* * *

Here an attack of lumbago, there a week-long migraine,
In March there's gastritis, in April—arterial stricture,
as for teeth or the flu, it's too much trouble to explain,
one after the next, your whole life through, that's the general picture.

It's interesting, though, how illness jumps all around your system,
one follows another, but they never unite as a single force—
this just hints of how it will go with your organism
when everything comes at once—death, of course.

What's this—my heart? You ticked away like a clock, adieu!
Brains, in you the world seethed as in a funnel!
Stomach—you connoisseur of still-lifes all in drops of dew!
Say good-bye, bronchial tubes, to winds through flute and tunnel!

It really is a pity, though, you've been a truly faithful team,
nourished by your very own ores and fonts,
so perfect the woven fabric, so finely sewn the seam,
that you even bore both soul and name, once.

Червь

Ты чей портрет рисуешь, червь,
скользя по слякоти на чреве?
Лица в нем нет, есть сумма черт
всего, чья плоть—земля и черви.

Уж не Вселенной ли самой
с луной, покрытой нежной слизью,
червь!—до которой по прямой
на глаз три пяди—только высью,

а ты—внизу. Но что есть высь?
Помпейской чашки рыхлый кобальт,
откуда вдоволь напились
зрачки чернил, а он всё копит,

и в то же время жирный прах
голубку поглощает сизу
с зерном руды на коготках—
как это видит зренье снизу.

Овраг, овраг переползти,
с холма на холм, ну пусть овражек,
след оставляя по пути,
след сжатий, судорог, растяжек,

жизнь растворяя и творя
на земляном ее отрезке,
червь, не ленись—чтоб штрих червя
проволочить по влажной фреске!

Worm

Whose portrait are you drawing, worm,
as on your womb you slide through sludge?
It has no face, at most a sum
of traits whose flesh is earth and worms.

Perhaps the Universe itself,
its moon all slick with tender slime
and just three fingerwidths away
(it seems), oh worm! But it's above,

and you're below. So what is height?
A Pompei teacup's crumbling cobalt—
inky pupils drank their fill
from it, and yet it's brimming still,

while at the same time fatty ash
is swallowing a blue-grey dove,
a grain of ore grasped in her claws—
as vision sees it from below.

O crawl across, across the gorge,
or cleft at least, from knoll to knoll,
and leaving in your trail a trace
of cramps, convulsions and extensions,

resolving and restoring life
within the earthen plane, oh worm,
don't stop, but keep on drawing strokes
of worm along a dewy fresco.

Городской пейзаж сто лет спустя

Синий, холодный, резкий над водой мускулистой
ветер, окончен розыск! Трепетную вакханку
ты потерял навеки, угомонись, не рыскай
здесь, где цирк Чинизелли торсом теснит Фонтанку.

Нет больше грешной, ветер, нет бежавшей за угол
в шали скользкого шелка, в шляпе черного фетра,
ни в стороне от сверстниц, ни одной, ни с подругой—
в жгучих твоих объятьях, в майских объятьях ветра.

Нет покаянной, горькой, нет прихожанки верной
Симеона-и-Анны, кротко, покорно, гордо
сжавшей и растянувшей, как трехпролетной фермой,
мост между Нет и Было воплем мук и восторга.

Нет больше хрупкой ветки, нет больше гибкой змейки,
раковины, поющей чем звучней, тем спокойней,—
есть этот мост в сиянье майски слепящей смерти
между площадью людной и пустой колокольней.

Плакать не надо, ветер, время ее минуло.
Ставь не на человека, ставь на моря и земли—
или на полдень, полный свежести, блеска, гула,
когда львы и гимнасты входят в цирк Чинизелли.

Portrait of St. Petersburg after a Century

You blue, you cold wind, sharp over muscular water,
call off your search! You've lost your trembling Bacchante
once and for all—calm down, stop ransacking this spot
where the Chinizelli Circus bellies against the Fontanka.

Gone the sinner, wind, she who vanished round the corner
in her black felt hat, in her slippery silk shawl,
not apart from her companions, or alone, or with a girlfriend—
in your searing embraces, in your May wind thrall.

Gone the repentant, the bitter, the faithful parishioner
of Simeon-and-Anna, meekly, submissively, proudly
compressed and extended, like a thrice-arched girder,
a bridge between Not and Was in a wail of torments and rapture.

Gone that delicate branch, gone the sinuous snake,
the singing shell, her voice more calm as its sound grew fuller—
only the bridge exists in the May-like glare of blinding death
between a bustling square and an empty cathedral tower.

Quiet your crying, wind, her time's gone by.
Lay your stake not on man, but on bodies of earth and water,
or stake on a noon full of freshness, buzzing and glaring bright
as the doors of the Circus open, and the lions and acrobats enter.

9 мая

Бабка моя, именем Соня,
не похороненная в блокаду,
духом муки и дров в межсезонье
вдруг пролетает по Ленинграду—

в сторону Луги и дальше на Ригу,
в атомах кремния, серы, железа,
к вою смотревшего ту корриду
глухонемого юрода-леса,

к выцветшим пятнам, к атомам угля,
к дюнам, где дождь—мулине рукоделья,
а облачка—взбитые букли
бабки моей, именем Бейля,

не похороненной после расстрела.
Так я, по крайней мере, увидел
их, когда "в землю отъидешь" подпела
хору старушка на панихиде.

May 9

My granny, who most knew simply as Sonya,
who lay unburied in the blockade,
her fragrance of flour and woodsmoke out of season
suddenly drifts over Leningrad—

heading for Luga and onward to Riga,
in atoms of silicon, sulphur and iron,
toward the wailing witness of that corrida,
that deaf-and-dumb idiot forest of wire,

toward stains now faded, toward atoms of coal,
toward dunes rain embroiders with delicate patterns,
and clouds fluffing into the ringlets and curls
of a woman called Beyla, also my granny,

who lay unburied after they shot her.
At least this is how they came into my head
as an old lady near me joined with the choir
for "ashes to ashes," singing the mass for the dead.

* * *

В пустой витрине—флакон духов "буржуа",
"аромат орхидеи 24".
Это они, когда была ты жива
путали мозг мой и хребта не щадили.

Это они пробирали плоть до кости,
пробуя над создателем власть изделий.
Это они, их молекулы, а не ты
пахли нигде не выросшей орхидеей.

Кто ты была? Я имя твое забыл—
не потому, что мщу,—потому что в мире
нет больше мира, твой питавшего пыл,
благоухавший эссенцией 24.

Страсть, обрываясь, не оставляет шва,
только рот пересохший и воздух спертый,
из инстинктов—озноб, из имен—"буржуа",
синий прозрачный куб с пробкой притертой.

* * *

An empty shop window. A bottle of "Bourgeois" perfume,
"Fragrance of Orchids #29."
This was the thing, when you were not yet gone,
clouding my brain and unsparing to the spine.

Testing the power of made over maker,
this penetrated clear to the bone,
this, its molecules, and not you, but the vapor
of an orchid never, anywhere, grown.

What was your name? I've forgotten who you were—
not in revenge, but in this world's absence
of the world that nourished your ardour,
aromatic with #29's essence.

Passion, cut short, leaves no ragged edge,
just unbreathable air and a mouth dry as paper,
of instincts—a chill; of all names—"Bourgeois,"
a blue transparent cube with a ground glass stopper.

* * *

Толе

Подушечкой пальца придавишь на скрипке струну,
как шкет подбираясь чутьем сквозь обертку к гостинцу,
объявишь: "Ну, Гайдн. Ну, не знаю. Да мало ли, ну,"—
и время пойдет убегать от большого к мизинцу.

Всё что-то мурлыкал, по хвое бродя и песку,
в стране, где парламент глухим обсуждается бором,
где бриз нагоняет, потом разгоняет тоску,
где то лишь история, что распевается хором.

Но звуки—стволов, насекомых, пернатых братья—
в компании сосен и птичек и пчел верховодя,
от крон до корней волокном древесины пройдя,
и до отзывались подзола, и соль мелководья.

Смычок тебе правую сложит в щепоть, а струна
на левой раскроет щепоть—так смотри, не заныкай
ту пьесу, не Гайдна, а то ли на М, то ли на—
неважно,—где двое вдоль моря идут за черникой.

Каприччо черничное, старый черничный концерт,
забыв про чернильные ноты, экспромтом, ну как-то,
забыв про страну, где позвякивал молот о серп,
ведь ты мне сыграешь? Черничное то пиццикато.

to Tolya

The pads of your fingers press down on the violin string,
like a kid bent on filching the candy he scents through the wrapper;
you announce, "Well, Haydn. I guess, I don't know, whatever you
                        think,"—
and now comes the time for your fingers to run from index to pinky.

You kept purring along, while strolling on needles and sand
in a land where a dense copse of pines discusses elections,
where the breeze catches up to and chases off feelings of longing
and where history's only the sung-in-unison selections.

But the sounds—of tree trunks, insects, and the feathered crowd—
lording over their company—pines, bees, and swallows,
coursing from crown to roots in a fiber of wood, are echoed
in the slanting "re" of the sun and the "sol" absorbed in the shallows.

The bow folds your right hand into a pinch, but the string
in your left lays the pinch open wide—so don't hide what this piece is:
this isn't Haydn, it starts with an M, or maybe with—
no matter, where two walk along by the sea, blackberry-picking.

A blackberry capriccio, an old blackberry concerto,
forgetting the black-inked notes, impromptu, well, somehow,
forgetting a country where hammer clinked against sickle,
will you just play for me? A blackberry pizzicato.

Ранний сбор ягод

С опереженьем на добрый месяц проходит лето,
еще июль, а леса сентябрьское сыплют семя.
Ветер восточный с дождем шумнут, что наложат вето,
но, хлопнув дверью, с опереженьем умчится время.

Что же спасет? Говорят, простота, в простоте смиренье:
как Иван-дурачок, в июле ходить по бруснику,
не думать о снеге, держать вверх ногами книгу,
снять с ходиков стрелки и спрашивать "скоко время?"

Но время уходит—ух! ах! уходит!—
опережая себя самое и всё на свете.
Год в три годика—год, год в 30—годик,
в 60—неделька: снег до субботы и мысль о лете.

А лето проходит с опереженьем на добрый месяц,
и в небе месяц с ножом в кармане, и я бруснику
спешу собрать, к лунному мху головою свесясь,
и вместе с падающей росой роняю ресницу.

Болгуновский лес

32

Early Berry-Picking

Outpacing itself by a good month, summer is fleeting,
though still July, the forests, September-like, strew their seed.
Together the east wind and rain mutter about a veto,
but time, already slamming the door, runs ahead at full speed.

What will save us? They say, simplicity—therein lies meekness:
like Ivan the Fool, to go cranberry-picking in July,
not thinking of snow, hold your book upside down,
snatch the hands off the village clock, and ask, "What time?"

But time just keeps going, and going, and going,
outpacing its own self and all earthly things.
A three-year-old's year is a year; at thirty it's short,
at sixty—six days of snow and a thought about summer.

And summer is fleeting, outpacing itself by a good month:
the crescent moon hangs in the sky with a knife in its pocket,
I rush to pick cranberries, head looming over the lunar moss
and together with the falling dew, I let an eyelash drop.

Bolgunovsky Forest

* * *

О. Димитрию

В лучшей части души, то есть в части, пустой
от чудных интересов и нервного чувства,
к чистой жизни он был предназначен, к святой,
то есть к знанью, сомненье которому чуждо.

В остальной же, больной, худшей части души,
мимолетными фактами мира набитой,
он любил запах сена и даже духи,
то есть мир, но как будто немного забытый,

то есть русские книги, где косят луга,
и немецкий концерт со щеглом и гобоем,
и парижскую живопись, скажем, Дега.
О, как слушал, смотрел, как читал он запоем!

Что ж худого? А то, что—не лучшая часть.
Что, душой от кромешного воя и стужи
отходя, лучшей части он здесь и сейчас
жить мешал, чтобы худшей не сделалось хуже.

Зла, однако, не вспомнит, спасаясь, душа:
худшей частью шепнет неуверенно: "Боже..?" —
и, на выходе свет за собою туша,
лучшей частью поймет и утешит: "Похоже".

34

* * *

to Father Dmitrii

In the best part of his soul, that is, the part devoid
of quirky fascinations and nervous flights of feeling,
his destiny was purity of living, saintliness,
that is, a knowledge to which all doubt is foreign.

In what was left, the unwell, worst part of his soul,
abundantly equipped with fleeting facts about the world,
he loved the scent of hay and even of perfume,
that is, the world, but as if only half-recalled,

that is, the fresh-cut fields in Russian books,
a German Konzertstück for reeds and finches,
Parisian paintings of, let's say, Degas—
How avidly he drank it in with all his senses!

And where's the harm in this? Only that it's not the best part. Only that,
withdrawing from that frozen Dark where wails intersperse
with gnashings, he kept his better part from living in the here and now
in order that the worst part not get even worse.

The soul, however, as it's saved, will recollect no evil—
The worst part is uncertain: "Lord?" he'll tentatively say,
and standing at the threshold, blowing out the light,
the better part will understand, and comfort him: "It looks that way."

Притча о неблудном сыне

Н.С.

Жизнь—это зеркало с отраженьем кого-то,
кем ты не стал, а мог бы, ну, скажем, вóра
или танцора, взявшего твои черты,
твой негатив: ты—анти-он, он—анти-ты.

Он—кем хотел, тем был. Ты хотел быть добрым,
между "нельзя" и "можно" занявшись торгом.
Он же пустился во вся, чуть не спился,
жизнь промотал—"если можно, зачем нельзя?"

Зеркало это—наследство от отчего брака
сыну неблудному с внешностью блудного брата,
чтоб доказать ваше тождество, а не родство.
Не обижайся, что ты не счастливей его.

Не обижайся—зеркало. И не отчайся:
счастье—всегда не твое; твое же счастье—
зрение, нервный к хребту от хрусталика путь,
не на себя реакция, а на ртуть.

Жизнь—это счастье видеть стекло согретым
кровью, дыханьем, просто—внезапным портретом
отца,—сквозь линзы влаги, омывшей глаза,
не узнавая его двоящегося лица.

Parable of the Elder Son

To N. S.

Life is a mirror reflecting somebody's face,
someone you didn't become—a robber, say,
or a dancer who snitched your features full-view,
your negative: you're anti-he; he's anti-you.

He became who he wanted to be. You meant to be good,
breathlessly working out trades between "mustn't" and "may."
He tried everything out, damned near turned into a sot,
squandered his life—"If 'may' is okay, why not?"

This mirror is the father's conjugal legacy
to an elder son who looks like his prodigal brother
to prove not kinship but common identity.
Don't mind that you're no happier than he.

Don't resent the mirror. And don't despair:
happiness isn't for you; your happiness
follows the nerve from the lens to the spinal column,
is not your reflex but the mirror's reflection.

Life is the happiness of seeing glass warmed
by blood and breath, by simply the sudden form
of your father seen through lenses of moisture that laved
your eyes, which didn't recognize his doubling face.

Из рецептов сна

… by a sleep to say we end
The heartache and the thousand natural shocks …
Hamlet

С сердцебиеньем проснешься под утро—сразу отпей
из чашки, поставленной с вечера в изголовье;
беззлобно в вороний кашель и оттепельную капель
вдышись, как в ритм, еще не увязший, по счастью, в слове.

А если вчерашний день или близкий друг
придут на память, подумай: "Господи Иисусе",
и снова: "Господи", и ни на шаг за круг
выдохов этих, вдохов, повторов, глотков не суйся.

В конце концов, сердцебиенье—всего лишь дубль
неудающихся сцен, сцен торжества и неги.
Руку на грудь, влаги еще пригубь,
и, чуть не забыл, все это время—сомкнуты веки.

На воду и воздух минимум мышц потрать,
минимум мозга на мысль, ибо ночь—охрана
от жизни. Пить, дышать, повторять—
да. А жизнь, как кадр со слепого экрана,

пусть на глазное плоско ложится дно—
кадр из фильма, в котором так и не снялся,—
бестелесней чаинки и перышка, как на сукно
чистое, вверх картинкой, карта пасьянса.

From Prescriptions for Sleep

> *… by a sleep to say we end*
> *The heartache and the thousand natural shocks …*
> Hamlet

You wake in the small hours with a racing heart—right away take a sip
from the cup you set last evening on the headboard;
breathe in, good-naturedly, the corvine cough and thawed-out drip
of snow, like a rhythm, fortunately not yet bound up in a word.

And if the day before or a close friend
should come to mind, think, "Lord Jesus," and again:
"O Lord," and don't venture a single step outside the circle
made by exhalation, inhalation, swallow, repetition.

For a racing heart is no more than an unsuccessful take
of certain scenes, languorous or festive.
Hand to your breast; from your cup—one more taste,
and, I almost forgot, all this with closed eyelids.

Spend a minimum of muscle on water and air,
a minimum of brain on thought, for night is your defense
against life. Drink, breathe, repeat—
yes. But life, like an exposure on a sightless screen

(let it lie flat at the back of your eye),
an exposure from a film you didn't even take part in,
is more bodiless than a plumelet or a flake of tea, like a card,
face-up on the clean, green felt, in a game of patience.

* * *

Я знал четырех поэтов.
Я их любил до дрожи
губ, языка, гортани,
я задерживал вздох,
едва только чуял где-то
чистое их дыханье.
Как я любил их, боже,
каждого из четырех!

Первый, со взором Леля,
в нимбе дождя и хмеля,
готику сводов и шпилей
видел в полете пчел,
лебедя—в зеве котельной,
ангела—в солнечной пыли,
в браке зари и розы
несколько букв прочел.

Другой, как ворон, был черен,
как уличный воздух, волен,
как кровью, был полон речью,
нахохлен и неуклюж,
серебряной бил картечью
с заброшенных колоколен,
и френч его отражался
в ртути бульварных луж.

Третий был в шаге лёгок,
в слоге противу логик
летуч, подлёдную музыку
озвучивал наперед
горлом—стройней свирели,
мыслью—пружинней рыбы,
в прыжке за золотом ряби
в кровь разбивающей рот.

* * *

I knew a quartet of poets.
I loved them to the very
trembling of lips, tongue, larynx,
I'd draw my breath in a little more,
even barely sensing somewhere
the cleanness of their breathing.
Lord how I loved them,
each one of these four.

The first, with his gaze of Pan,
in a nimbus of hops and rain,
saw Gothic spires and canopies
in the flight of bees on their rounds,
In the boiler-room's maw—a swan,
An angel in the dust of a solar breeze.
In a rose's marriage with sunrise
he wrote some letters down.

The second was black, like a raven,
like air from the street, he was open,
and full, as with blood, with chatter.
Ruffled up and hunkered down,
his silver gunshot scattered
from a broken bell-tower,
and his field-jacket glinted in mercury
pools on the avenues' dun.

Light of step, the third one flew
full in the face of logic
in style, and sounded his music
in advance, encased in ice.
His throat—slimmer than a reed-pipe,
his thought suppler than the fish
who, springing at gold in a ripple,
bloodies its mouth with its tries.

Был нежен и щедр последний,
как зелень после потопа,
он сам становился песней,
когда по ночной реке
пускал сиявший кораблик
и, в воду входя ночную,
выныривал из захлёба
с жемчугом на языке.

....

Оркестр не звучней рояля,
рояль не звучней гитары,
гитара не звонче птицы,
поэта не лучше поэт:
из четырех любому
мне сладко вернуть любовью
то, что любил в начале.
То, чего в слове нет.

The last one was tender and giving
like verdure after the Flood.
As he launched a small, bright ship
on a river immersed in night,
he himself transformed into song
and entering that night water,
he emerged from a choking splutter,
a pearl on his tongue.

....

A quartet sounds not more than piano,
piano not more than guitar,
guitar not more vibrant than birdsong,
one poet not more than the rest.
For me the pleasure's proved
in returning to friends with love
what I loved in our beginning
what a word fails to express.

* * *

М.Я.

Надеваю на сердце, на грозди желез
свод хребта, из ключиц и из ребер каркас:
миг—и корни притерлись, и сердце вжилось
в стебель торса, хотя был прикинут на глаз.

Надеваю рубаху, лелею тепло
коченеющей кожи, нагого плеча:
миг—и тело к льняным рукавам приросло,
и пора уже прятать их в крылья плаща.

И тогда, под одеждой нахохлясь, как дрозд,
остается напяливать сверху избу
вместе с ветром над крышей, бросаемым в дрожь
перед тем, как он сумеркам сдастся и сну.

Вот теперь и скажи-ка себе самому,
что такое душа, если все это дом
и желанье его—только кутаться в тьму
всем узором спасенным нутра, всем нутром.

* * *

to M. Ya.

I pull on over my heart, over bunches of glands
a spine's arch, a collar-bone carcass with ribs:
in a moment the roots have set and the heart has joined
the torso's stem, which it had already sized up.

I pull on a shirt, trying to save some heat
in my numb, shivering skin, my bare shoulder:
in a moment the body has stuck to the linen sleeves
and it's time to hide them under a poncho.

Then, wriggling under the clothes like a thrush,
it's time to pull the house on over my head
along with the wind passing the roof in a rush
before it yields to the twilight and falls asleep.

So now tell yourself truly what lies in your heart,
if all of this house and wanting a home
is only wrapping yourself in the dark
with a pattern saved from inside, yours alone.

Песенка

Когда мне было десять лет,
мир потерял впервые прелесть:
я думал, милиционер
меня нечаянно застрелит.

Когда мне стало двадцать лет
и я обкуривался Ницше,
я знал, с другими уцелев,
что нас зарежут коммунисты.

Когда мне стало тридцать лет,
я перестал бояться внешних,
но ждал, когда, напав на след,
меня задушит кагебешник.

Вокруг был город Ленинград,
и царь, скача на дальний берег,
наставил конский медный зад
на исаакиевский скверик,

а справа, где сыра земля
под складом величаво-грязным,
шел—позади с еще двумя—
немолодой мужчина в красном,

и хоронилась за стеной,
как на картине у Симоне
Мартини, с книжкой записной
в руке и с дырочкой в короне,

вполоборота вся от пят
до темени, в плаще с запахом,
теперь, когда мне шестьдесят,
пришедшая на место страхам.

A Little Song

When I was just a boy of ten,
the world first lost its fascination:
I thought that a militia man
would accidentally blow my brains out.

When I survived to twenty years,
enveloped in the fumes of Nietzsche,
I knew, together with my peers,
the communists would slit our windpipes.

At thirty years, I ceased to be
afraid of what the world could threaten,
but waited for the KGB
to find my trail and stop my breathing.

And all around was Leningrad,
and having gained the distant shore,
the tsar now aimed his steed's bronze back
toward St. Isaac's garden square,

and to the right the earth was raw
beneath a stately, filthy storehouse,
and just past that a man in red,
no longer young, walked with two others,

and like a painting by Simone
Martini—in her hands her notebook,
a tiny torn place in her crown,
half-twisted from her heels to hair-roots,

her long coat tucked about her well—
the one who came to where my fears
had been for all these sixty years
is hidden now beyond the wall.

Мне с ней—нам было … Боже мой,
да Ты нас знаешь. Время било
себя, как моль. Сам свет был моль.
Был день. Был хлеб. Был страх. Мне было.

Time, moth-like, beat against itself …
With her—we were … My God, You know us.
And even light as moth-beats fell.
And day was, bread was, fear … and I was.

На смерть

Автомобиль останавливается у сада,
по сигналу из дома распахиваются ворота,
вспугнутая лиса через каменную ограду
прыгает. Это и есть Европа.

Круг тем за чаем привычный, привычно узкий:
во-первых, бездарный Париж; во-вторых и в-третьих,
Тель-Авив и Нью-Йорк, дикарство. И так как русский
присутствует, речь заходит о гиперборейцах.

Де, медведеподобны. А что творится
на север и юг от экватора! Скоро все потемнеем.
А это правда, что в Петербурге была царица,
называвшая одного европейца Энеем?

И тут все вспоминают, зачем собрались:
что человека, чей череп и ребра подобны Риму,
а сердце с каждым рассветом глотает радость
великой жизни, выбросило на берег Леты, как рыбу.

Разговор продолжается, но спазмом на спазме,
как будто действие перебирается за кулисы.
Тело героя лежит на постели в роскошной спальне.
В сумеречной аллее играют лисы.

On the Death of ***

An automobile pauses in the garden;
on a signal from the house, the gates open up,
spooking a fox, which easily clears a low stone wall
and disappears. This is truly Europe.

At tea, the usual topics, usually confined:
First, about fatuous Paris; second and next after that,
Tel Aviv and New York: barbaric. And since a Russian
is present, the Hyperboreans come up in the chat:

They were like bears … But what's brewing now above
and below the equator? We're headed for the built-in tan …
And wasn't there a Petersburg tsaritsa who gave
the name "Aeneas" to a certain European man?

And here they're reminded of why they gathered:
a man whose skull and ribs are like Rome, whose heart fills
at each dawn with joy for life in its greatness,
has been flung to Lethe's further shore, like a fish.

The conversation continues, but spasm by spasm,
as if the action were moving behind what they're saying.
The hero's body lies on its bed in a sumptuous bedroom.
In a twilit lane foxes are playing.

* * *

Чтоб мотыльки ресниц, и просто мотыльки,
и стайка струн и флейт, ни весело, ни скорбно
вспорхнувших, и сирень, дохнувшая "не лги"
трепещущему рту и перехвату горла,

чтобы тебя, полип, чтоб, чувственная слизь,
они тебя, комок, замес слюны и пыли,
тебя, почти никто, тебя, почти не жизнь,
чтобы тебя, почти не вещество, любили,

попробуй сам любить—не просто не обидь,
а непонятно как, в немыслимом усилье,
без радости, без слов, попробуй их любить,
бессмысленных, тебе чужих, сложивших крылья.

* * *

These eyelash butterflies, and simply butterflies,
and flocks of strings and flutes, neither gay nor sad
as they take flight, and lilacs breathing out "Don't lie,"
to trembling mouth and catching in your throat,

in order that these love you—you, a polyp, slime
of feeling, you, a hump of clay, of spit and dust,
you, almost not alive, to have them love you,
who barely counts as substance, as molecules of matter,

try loving them yourself, although you don't know how,
not simply not offending, with unimagined effort,
without a word, or joyousness, try loving them
these foolish, foreign things, whose wings have folded now.

* * *

Когда дымящийся, сырой,
когда парящий в высших сферах,
когда палач мой, мой герой,
мой труп, когда, короче, эрос

приходит в драповом пальто,
гримасой смеха, рыжей стрижкой,
опроверженьем кто есть кто,
прихрамыванием, припрыжкой,

когда в атласную берет
обтяжку он шатер скелета,
когда иглой сшивает рот—
стежок, стежок—и вы калека:

тогда весь мир—театр зверей,
и, значит, лишний темп проделан,
и лед долбящая форель
не рыба, не душа, а демон

там, где ни тела, ни лица,
ни голоса, где тонус поднят
той ткани, чей состав нельзя
ни позабыть потом, ни помнить,

где тяга вся—к труду, к труду,
и, день и ночь породу роя,
кровь добывают, как руду
из пульпы негашеной крови.—

И ради этого—ты?! Ты!
Невероятно. Или верность
себе—тебя, твои черты
выбрасывает на поверхность,

Eros

When raw and ready, cold and steaming,
when soaring through the upper ether,
when my hangman, my grand hero,
my dead body, in a word when Eros

shows up in a thick wool coat,
a grin on his face, a carrot hair-do,
to Who's Who a living antidote,
with a limp when he wants, a leap when he cares to,

when he stretches satin tightly
over the framework of my bones,
when his needle sews my mouth unsightly—
stitch, stitch—and I'm a crone,

then all the world's the animals' stage,
and the super pace has been worked out,
and the trout that's memorizing ice
is not a fish or soul but a devout

devil where there's no body, face
or voice, where now the tone is raised
of that tissue whose make-up can't be placed
to be remembered or erased,

where all the pull's toward work, more work,
and day and night digging genes,
the blood brings up a sort of ore
from the pulp of quick-limed seams.—

And just for this—you do it? You!
Most unlikely. Or does being true
to yourself toss you and all your features
in with superficial creatures

как ската, чтоб столкнуть круги
и рябь? И, дергаясь, лепеча,
настичь внезапно ритм *руки*,
месящей тесто человечье.

like a sting-ray to make ripples band
with rings? Twitching, lisping, you suddenly find
you catch the rhythm of the *hand*
kneading the dough of humankind.

* * *

Елене

Хочешь, можно и в Риме жить, как не в Риме,
а, положим, в Крыму или в той же Риге—
жарить рыбу, гнать за окно тоску.
Надо для этого только быть нелюбимым
целой планетой и особенно Римом.
Ты-то любим? Я-то да—но рискну.

Первое—зрительному не поддамся зуду.
Разморожу треску, перемою посуду;
в лавке куплю батарейку к часам;
в ларьке газетном взгляну, как там Рома—Парма,
вничью? И даже если флюиды шарма
вдохну—то по собственной воле, сам.

Шарм, я имею в виду, валянья на койке,
или езды в зоосад с вокзала на "тройке".
А почему, вы спросите, в зоосад?
Да просто там ни истории нет, ни римлян—
а вокзал демонстрирует, что лишь искривлен,
но не закрыт путь чужаку назад.

В принципе, и вздремнуть на скамейке в парке
можно; и в церкви уставиться на огарки;
можно и на себя в стёклах витрин—
с тем, чтоб признать, что эти морщины, руины,
хочешь не хочешь, в холмы посреди равнины
встраиваются—и проступает Рим.

* * *

to Elena

You can, if you like, live even in Rome as not in Rome,
but, let's suppose, the Crimea or plain old Riga—
chase *ennui* out the window, roast a fish.
For this you only have to be unloved
by all the planet and especially Rome.
And you—are you loved? I am, but I'll risk it.

The first thing: I'll not yield to visual itches.
I'll thaw out some cod, re-wash the dishes;
a battery for my watch at the store, a glance at the shelf
for the news—what was the score in Rome-vs.-Parma—
a draw? And even if I breathe in that charm,
that fluid—it'll be of my own will, myself.

By charm, I have in mind a camp bed to loaf on,
or a trip on the "3" to the zoo from the station.
And why the zoo, you'd like to be informed?
Because you'll find no history there, or Romans—
and the station proves that for no man
is the way back barred—it's just deformed.

In principle, you could even drowse on a park bench,
and find a place in a church for a candle-end;
and in shop-window glass catch your own view—
if you accept that these wrinkles, and ruins,
like it or not, are building to mounds on their plains—
and, imperceptibly, Rome is seeping through.

* * *

Пропой, синица, два колена
про жизнь без плена, жизнь без плена,
вспорхни и прозвени, артист,
про царство семени и снега,
в котором альфа и омега—
полет и свист, полет и свист.

* * *

Sing two figures, chickadee,
of life set free, of life set free,
Take wing, ring out with purest skill,
about a realm of snow and seed,
where alpha and omega meet,
Fly up and trill, fly up and trill.

СОФЬЯ

Софье полтора года

Из места, о котором
                            мы ничего не знаем
и называем раем, является дитя,
дух молока и яблока под царским горностаем,
иной природы нежели кузены и братья:

из шелка и фарфора его состав изваян,
на сотню дней рассчитан двойного бытия,
волной воздушной сплюснут, небесным верен стаям—
а дышит тем, что выдохнут иных природ тела.

И, к ним мало-помалу клонясь, приноровляясь,
дней зá сто постигает, что этих тел любовь,
хоть не сравнима с тамошней, не к месту и не в радость,
но не за так им, грубым, дается, а за боль.

Ну что ж, любовь убога, но и за ту спасибо—
жить—это жить, таращась, а не в цветах бродя.
Тем более, что чтó там? лицо?—оно красиво.
Ну что ж, давайте пробовать, кузены и братья!

....

И ты оттуда тоже, творенье Божье Соня:
еще курится ладан и мак вокруг тебя,
еще ты засыпаешь при звездах и при солнце—
но спишь уже по-нашему—вздыхая и сопя.

SOPHIA

Sophie Is Eighteen Months

From a place
                   about which we know absolutely nothing
and designate as heaven, a little child has arrived,
the soul of milk and apples in royal ermine clothing,
of a different nature from all our brothers and our relatives.

Of silk and porcelain is his figure well composed,
designed to last a double life a hundred days,
layered with air waves, faithful to celestial flocks,—
inhaling what the different-nature bodies exhale.

Little by little inclining toward them, going with them,
the hundred days gone by, he grasps that the love these bodies have
though unlike what's all around them, is joyless and uncertain,
but that's not from what things work for them, the vulgar—it's
                   from pain.

Well, so, love's a pauper, but thanks for what is there—
living is keeping your eyes open, not meandering in flowers.
All the more because what's that? A face? Lovely and fair.
So, let's see what we can do, relatives and brothers!

....

You, too, come from there, heavenly creature Sophie:
the incense and the poppy seed still burns around you,
still you fall asleep in starlight and in sunlight—
but sleeping you breathe noisily through your nose as we do.

63

Здесь всё не так. Всё тянет обратно, тянет в лоно—
Эдема, Авраама, долины, где цвело,
на поле, где сияло, где жило до излома,
который сердце вылущил и чистое чело.

Откуда же ты, Софья? Чего меня лишает
твое забвенье? Или хоть малого стебля
еще ты помнишь ласку, хоть очерк тех лужаек?
А то с чего гляжу я с восторгом на тебя!?

Here everything's off kilter, strains backward, longs for the lap
of Eden, of Abraham, the valley where everything flourished,
the field where everything shimmered with life before the great snap
that shelled the heart and lopped the ingenuous brow.

So, Sophie, where are you really from? Do I lose a lot
because of your unconsciousness? Perhaps you recall
the caress of a little stalk, or what those meadows looked like?
Why else would I be looking at you in rapture and awe?

Младенцу

На-ка охапку ромашек—
просто за то, что люблю,—
равных по алгебре нашей
желтому с белым нулю.

Или примерь, раз уж гладью
вышито платье, жасмин:
веткой вплетется на свадьбу
в лиф, а завянет—простим.

Не выплавлять же из бронзы
к шраму губных лепестков
льнущую свастику розы,
видимую в телескоп,

то есть гвоздями тычинок,
вбитыми в корень креста,
вновь ковыряться в причинах,
чья и зачем красота

в аксонометрии тюрем,
в печени черной, в тоске,
в том, что где гвозди, там Дюрер
бьет молотком по доске.

Вот оно, начал о здравье—
жди, что снесет в упокой:
что подарю, сам и граблю
той же дарящей рукой,

жизнь проводя в разговорах.
В общем, ромашку, жасмин,
клевер—держи-ка весь ворох:
ангел, ты справишься с ним.

To an Infant

Here's an armful of daisies—
simply because I love you—
making, the way we do math now,
a yellow and white zero true.

Or when you've a satin-stitched dress,
try on a jasmine bouquet:
the wedding sprig sewn in your bodice
will wilt—we allow it; that's its way.

No point casting in bronze
for the scar of your petalled lips
a clinging swastika rose
as seen through a telescope,

that's to say, using stamens like nails
driven into the root of a cross,
to go rummaging through the reasons
why there's beauty—and whose—

in the axonometry of jails,
in black bile, in nostalgia,
in the fact that where there are nails
Dürer hammers away.

The point is, I set out talking 'health';
just wait till 'rest in peace' comes round:
what I'm giving you I myself
take back with my giving hand

by turning life into farewells.
In sum, the daisies and jasmine
and clover—keep the whole bunch:
angel, you'll manage fine.

Софье два с половиной

Зачехлив инстинкт, жизнь пошла на нерве,
всё чистоголосей, всё пышноволосей,
трепеща, как яхта перед спуском с верфи,—
и всё чаще Соню звать охота Зосей:

шаг—как лепет светский, лепет—как купанье
ню; размыта родина, в фокусе Варшава;
у ясновельможной ясноглазой пани
даже и младенчество в меру моложаво.

Я был тоже молод, Софья, ах, как молод!—
как бывает шляхта раз в столетье в Польше.
Жаль, уж не мурлычет твой роток, а молвит,
но и молвь—музыка, помни же и пой же.

Когда восемнадцать, когда двадцать минет,
вдруг мотив привяжется, вальс знакомо нервный,
и инстинкт из груды ту пластинку вынет,
сталью игл изрытую, шарма звук неверный.

Ах, какая прелесть этот хрупкий гонор,
этот зной манеры, все которым грелись!
Гордая ли слабость—ваш смертельный номер?
Нежная ли гордость—эта ваша прелесть?

Так давай же вместе ножкой, Соня, топнем
и заплачем вместе, чтоб к тебе вернулось
то, что между "знаем" прожито и "помним",
то, что, хочешь, мудрость будет, хочешь, юность.

Sophie Is Two and a Half

Slipcovering instinct, life took off on a dare,
the voice always purer, the hair always fuller,
all aquiver like a yacht before leaving its pier—
and more often the wish not be 'Sonya' but 'Zosya':

a step is grown-up palaver; palaver, a bath
all bare; home is wiped out—a trick Warsaw has done;
for such a clear-eyed, clearly old-family young lady
being an infant to some extent makes her look young.

I, too, was young, Sophie, oh so young!
as gentry in Poland are every hundred years.
Unfortunately, your little mouth no more hums
but speaks, yet speech, too, is music don't forget, and sing.

When eighteen comes, when twenty comes after that,
A *motif* suddenly gets you, a familiar, nervous waltz,
and instinct plucks the special record out,
the needles' pitted steel, the soft cheat of *charme*.

O how lovely is this fragile arrogance,
this sultry manner which has made everyone feel warm!
Has conceited weakness, then, your number on it?
Or sweet and tender pride—is that your charm?

So, Sophie, let's put our dancing feet together,
let tears come to us both so that you're returned
what happens between "we know" and "we remember,"
so, if you want, you're wise; if you want, young.

Софье три с половиной

Отражается то или се
на лице, как в зерцале,—но чистым,
как цветок, остается лицо,
обращенное к выцветшим лицам,
непричастное к этим и к тем,
всем сродни, ни на чье не похоже,
словно то, что есть солнце и тень,
все равно роговице и коже.

Все лицо—это лоб, крутизну
перенявший у бездны небесной,
но и щеки, наощупь волну
с водяной поделившие бездной,
но и губы, когда их слова
покидают, как звук, как улыбка,
как улитка домок, как пчела
сад, в который закрыта калитка.

Наконец, это глаз: как он щедр
тем, что сходства ему не додали,—
безмятежность чурается черт,
чистоте не присущи детали.
Не гляди же, как мы,—удержись
в полузнанье твоем бесподобном—
смыслом жизни стирается жизнь,
как любовь объясненьем любовным.

Sophie Is Three and a Half

Everything shows in the face
like a mirror, but like a flower
the face remains perfect in place,
turned toward the faces that faded,
uninvolved in any of them,
akin to all but like none,
the same as shadow and sun
indifferent to skin and cornea.

The face is: a forehead that pared
its slope from the dome of heaven,
and cheeks that by touch shared
a wave from the depths of the ocean,
and lips whose words fly out
as a sound or a smile, the way
a snail quits its house or a bee,
a garden whose gate has been shut.

And then there's the eye: capacious
in that no likeness ever was made—
tranquility skirts its features,
its purity wants no details.
Don't see things as we do—hang on
to the half-knowing mind of your own—
life is washed out by its meaning,
like love explained to the loved.

Колыбельная

Муха спит на потолке,
рыба спит на плавнике,
птица дремлет под крылом,
пес под письменным столом.

В центре неба спит звезда,
спит толпа туда-сюда,
поезд спит на всем ходу,
спит пчела в своем меду.

Спит овца с волчицей врозь—
вместе плохо им спалось,
спит зима белым-бела,
вся земля в постель легла.

Всех на свете клонит в сон,
спит на кафедре Джон Донн,
спят в церквах колокола,
спи, Джон Донн, твоя взяла.

Спи, Владимир Соловьев,
на перине мудрых слов,
больше их не тронь, не трать
на Софию, дай ей спать.

Спи, София—Соня, спи.
Перед сном сходи пипи,
в теплоту и мякоть ляг,
как лягушка и хомяк.

Слышит Бог твой сонный вздох,
сосчитай теперь до трех,
спи, как снег, трава и мышь—
тихо, тихо. Вот и спишь.

Lullaby for Sophie

Fish is sleeping, floating on his fin,
Fly is sleeping, sticking to the ceiling,
Bird is snoozing, head beneath her wing,
Rover's chasing rabbits in his dream.

Star is sleeping high up in the sky,
crowds are sleeping as they hurry by,
train is sleeping—don't you think it's funny?
bumble-bee is dozing in his honey.

Sheep and she-wolf have to sleep apart—
sleeping both together wasn't smart,
winter's sleeping wrapped up all in white,
all the earth lies snug in bed tonight.

Everyone is nodding off to sleep,
John Donne in his pulpit counting sheep,
church-bells in their towers sleep, John Donne,
go ahead and sleep, your side has won.

Rest, Vladimir Solov'yov, your head,
words of wisdom be your feather bed,
let your thoughts be, it's no use to keep
wasting them on Sophie, let her sleep.

Sleep, Sophie—Sophie, go to sleep.
First, though, go and brush your teeth and pee,
lie down in the warmth of your cocoon,
like the frog and hamster and racoon.

Sleepy breaths float up to God in heaven,
try to count now all the way to seven,
sleepy like a mouse, like grass and snow
hush-a-bye. And off to sleep you go.

Софье четыре с половиной

Давай пойдем погулять, а чтобы назад,
не заблудившись, вернуться, точней прицелься
словами в вещи, но не спеши назвать
бабочку золушкой—что как она принцесса?

Решай, то коза звенит или блеет комар—
имей в виду: то, что делается на пробу,
это навеки. Я, например, захромал,
потому что устал—а думал, ищу дорогу.

Давай, ты будешь журавль, я буду жираф—
высокий, пока на лазурь ты не сменишь глину;
или, давай, ты море, а я корабль,
гонящий волну параллельно птичьему клину.

Короче, ты будешь что-то, что лишь бегом
передвигалось в веках при рабынях и боннах,—
что-то, чье имя, дающееся испокон
времени, принадлежало и мне, Ребенок.

Sophie Is Four and a Half

Let's go take a walk, and in order to come back
without getting lost, aim your words better at things
but don't be in a hurry to label a butterfly
Cinderella—for what sort of a princess has wings?

Decide if a goat buzzes or a gnat bleats—
keep in mind: what gets worked out by trial and error
lasts forever. For example, I started dragging my feet
because I was tired, but I thought I was lost in a detour.

You be a crane, let's say, and I'll be a giraffe—
very tall provided you don't change clay into azure;
or, let's you be the sea and I'll be a sailing ship
chasing each wave like the wedge-shaped flight of a tern.

In short, you'll be something that traveled in double time
during centuries of slave maids and governess-nurses—
something whose name, existing from time immemorial,
belonged once on a time to me, too, Child.

Сонет

Ты, Софья, ляг, а я у изголовья
присяду, и давай поговорим.
А можно между первым и вторым
за ужином. А? Как ты смотришь, Софья?

Про что? Про все. Без всякого условья—
предмет любых бесед всегда незрим.
Пусть это будет рыба. Или Рим.
Пусть ангел. Или будущая Софья.

По-го-во-рим—понятно? Все равно,
ты, я, поочередно, заодно,
смысл, заумь—я не против пустословья.

Тут цель—твой голосок и слух твой. Дня
чтоб не было, когда тебе меня,
точнее, мне тебя не слышно, Софья.

Sonnet

You lie down, Sophie, and I'll sit here
on the bed; let's have a private conversation.
Or during supper, maybe, we could, between
the first and second courses. That a good idea?

What about? Everything. No pre-set recipe—
ahead of time, all topics are unknown.
Let's say it could be fish. Or maybe Rome.
Or angels. Or Sophie's promising career.

Let's have a chat—that clear? No matter
who's first, you or me, or both at once, or one after
another, or it doesn't make sense—I'm not against chatter.

The goal is to get you to speak and to train your ear.
May the day never come when you can't hear me,
Sophie, or more to the point, when it's you I can't hear.

Софье шесть лет

Не торопись во взрослые, взрослый глуп,
он под подушку не сунет молочный зуб,
а ляпнет "кальций". Он говорит всерьез,
где бы смеяться. А все потому что взросл.

Не повторяй за ними. Мильон их слов
прежде сопрел в мильоне других голов.
Взрослый всегда вспотел и всегда озяб—
перенимай закалку у снежных баб.

Что ты читаешь? Читай про принцесс и фей.
Принцы румяны, хотя голубых кровей.
Гномы бегают вкось и наперерез,
а взрослые—тонус поднять или сбросить вес.

Цвета лица у них два—бледен и смугл.
Взрослый не верит в одушевленье кукл.
Ты же своей щёки раскрась, чтоб ожила,
красным и синим, взбей кудри и кружева.

Взрослые утверждают, что жить любя
так, как ты любишь—всей полнотой себя,
после детства нельзя, наступает сбой,
ты становишься всеми, никто тобой.

Так или нет, останься Софьей еще. Напяль
что-нибудь взрослое на себя—туфли, шаль,
волосы под античных матрон расчеши.
И не спеши за возрастом, не спеши.

Sophie Is Six

Don't rush to grow up; grown ups are dumb;
they don't put their baby teeth out for the fairy to come
but blurt out "calcium." So serious, they never own up
they ought to laugh, too. And all because they're grown up.

Don't copycat them. Their millions of words are dead,
rotting for years in millions of other heads.
A grown up is always sweating or freezing to death—
toughen yourself the way a snowman gets tough.

What're you reading? Read about fairy princesses. I do.
Princes are ruddy-faced though their blood is blue.
Gnomes run every which way, always in haste,
but grown ups raise tone or get rid of weight.

Their faces come in two colors—swarthy and pale.
A grown up doesn't believe in the real life of dolls.
Paint the cheeks of yours red and blue to brighten her face
so she comes alive, and fluff up her curls and her lace.

Grown ups keep saying that living the way you want
to live now, completely full of yourself, you can't
when childhood's over and every shortcoming's true;
you become like everyone else; no one, like you.

So, one way or another, stay Sophie. Pull
on something grown-up—a pair of dress shoes, a shawl,
do your hair the way classical matrons did theirs,
and don't hurry, don't hurry, to add on any years.

Софье семь лет

Прощайте, первых семь! Пока,
глядевшая на все так зорко
и честно, что почти не горько
с тобой прощаться на века,
великолепная семерка.

Прощай. Теперь полудела
примнут тебя, полузаботы,
жизнь с теми пополам, кого ты
изобретешь сама. Была
ты—ты, теперь ты будешь кто-то.

Останется … —ну что? Огонь,
то «о!» в твоем зрачке (как в слове
«любовь») под convictион удареньем брови—
тот гревший мне семь лет ладонь
твой жар с температурой крови.

И в камере, за давний путч
отсиживая, дней на склоне
что помнить мне, как не в ладони
птенцом из сна влетевший луч,
семь лет носивший имя Сони?

Sophie Is Seven

Farewell, first seven. For now—so long,
you absolutely marvelous seven
that so tightly trained your beady eye
on everything that now it almost isn't sad
forever and ever to say good-by.

Farewell. Now you'll be taken up
with halfway things and halfway cares
and halfway living with all the selves
you yourself invent. Once upon a time
you were you; now you'll be Someone Else.

What will still be there? The fire in
the i-dot of your eyes (as round
as the "o" of "love") beneath the down
beat of your eyebrow, your impassioned blood
that for seven years warmed my palm.

And in my jail cell as my days decline,
sitting out an old-time *putsch*,
what should I remember but on my palm
a fledgling's dreamy light ray landing
that for seven years bore Sophie's name?

Софья пошла в школу

Флор и Лавр, мучч., 31 авг.
Святцы

Неприкаянная в мельтешенье толп,
на огромном крохотная дворе,
как теленок в тесный загон—топ-топ
дважды-двум учиться и точке-тире.

А поверх тополей, куполов и крыш
воронье на пустом Москвы этаже
черным бьет крылом, и не скажешь кыш,
потому что оно не из птиц уже.

На их ругань—втянутых в коловорот—
отзывается жалобный стон телят,
потому что кто в стае, всегда орет,
а которых школят, всегда скулят.

О, последнее Первое сентября,
ты взошло, и что теперь ни сентябрь,
то Софии в учетчики и писаря,
отцветя, сходить. Правда, Флор и Лавр?—

Флор и Лавр, разгневавшие царя,
под глушильный крик городских ворон
из колодца тесного говоря
о таком, чего ведать не ведал он.

Взгромоздив на плечики рюкзачок,
никогда не снимешь его уже.
Про что знаешь—молчок. Здесь идет в зачет—
что не знаешь. В бесчисленном тираже.

Sophie Has Started School

Flor and Laur, martyrs, Aug. 31
Church calendar

Bewildered and lost in the shuffle and glimmer of crowds,
a tiny thing in a vast expanse of yard,
like a calf tightly packed in a feed lot—pull-push,
to learn two times two and where to put period—dash,

while over the poplars, the domes and the roofs
on a vacant Moscow storey carrion crows
beat their black wings, you can't scare them off
because they're not like birds lined up in a row.

Their cursed cawing, bearing down like a drill,
provokes a pitiful moan from the kine,
(because anything in a flock always yells,
and whoever is schooled always whines).

O, recent September the First, you came
and went; now, September or not any more,
Sophie, her bloom faded, is on the way to become
a checker, a clerk. Right, Flor and Laur?—

Flor and Laur, who, jammed into a well
under the deafening cries of old city crows,
by whatever they said drove the tsar wild,
who wanted no part of what they made him know.

Now that your little backpack is on,
you won't take it off. Never. About what you
know—not a word. Here they work on
whatever you don't. In countless copies.

83

Баллада о черной карте

Я черную карту решил разыграть,
но те, с кем уселся за столик,
не поняли, крыть им ее или брать
и что она, черная, стоит.
А в ней-то одной и была вся игра,
невысканной годы и годы,
пропащей, сводящей на нет веера
из только что вскрытой колоды.
И все, что стояло у нас на кону,
того не будило азарта,
как эта, мной пущенная по сукну,
слепая последняя карта.

Я ставил, к примеру, на черный зрачок,
недвижный под вскинутой бровью,
он в мозг мой впивался и сердце мне жег
оплавленной сплющенной дробью;
а кто поумнее—на глаз целиком,
на карий, но тоже, как школьник,
который с предметом наслышкой знаком,
вправляя овал в треугольник;
а прочие—кто на себя, кто нá всех …

Но ставки—товары на рынке,
а это, как бездны зияющий зев,
лежала судьба без картинки,
как угля облатка, вобравшая гул
и риск рудника без ступеней.
И клети. И взгляд отрешенный тонул
в ее поглощающей тени.

The Ballad of the Black Card

The black card was the one I decided to play,
       but the people with me at table
didn't know whether to cover or call
       or what picking up black would enable.
How the game would turn out depended on it,
       for years and years very modest,
a pee-wee now undercutting the hands
       fanned out from the deck we'd just opened.
The whole pile of chips in the kitty before us
       didn't raise such a fuss and furor
as what I tossed out on the baize table cloth,
       sightless, my ultimate joker.

It was on the black pupil I placed my bet,
       on the raised brow's motionless spot;
it bore into my brain and stung my heart
       with an unalloyed angle shot;
like someone who's smarter choosing the eye,
       picking out and betting on hazel
like a schoolboy who's met the Great Seal by hearsay
       in a triangle fitting an oval;
like the others, some picking one color, some picking all …

       Jackpots are wares gone to market,
but here, like the yawning maw of a chasm,
       was fate without even a photo,
like a briquette of coal impounding the roar
       and the risk of a mine with no grade.
Or a cage. And the look of aloofness sank down
       in fate's all-devouring shade.

* * *

Что говорят к концу? Что земля есть плавное
тело. Что Рим и Иерусалим
не уступят один другому ее. Но главное,
что она организм, и он неделим.

Что еще? Что арбе, поворачивая,
ни на миг не сменить направленья колес,
и поэтому то, что в земле есть горячего,
роет две борозды по образчику слез.

Что же в ней есть холодного, то—гармония.
Стадо холмов и мышц посреди колоннад
ребер и рощ. Связь их всё церемоннее—
кожа скрывает жар, но сама холодна.

То—рудники и магма, а это—дерево,
сложенный, как собор и скала, кипарис,
для которого солнце, садясь, отмеривает
под колокольню верх и под шахту низ.

Стало быть, не обязательно, что что искусственно,
то неестественно. Просто жерло утрат,
свет поглощая, всхлип испускает—устное
слово, то самое, что к концу говорят.

Что говорят? Что говорят—то теряется
в шуме воздуха. Говорят, что земля
это пауза, и она повторяется,
как двойная прерывистая колея.

* * *

What can be said in drawing to a close? That the earth's
an undulate body, that Jerusalem and Rome
won't concede her one to the other, but first,
that she is an organism, indivisibly her own.

What else? That the roughest of carts, in turning,
won't change the wheels' direction even as it veers,
and for this reason what in the earth is burning
digs two furrows, of the type described by tears.

And the coldness in her is part of the harmony:
in among the colonnades of ribs and groves a fold
of hills and muscles bonded in ceremony—
the skin conceals the heat, but itself is cold.

That is magma and veins of ore, but this—a tree:
a cypress like a crag and a cathedral for which, already low,
the sun marks off the top part for a belfry
and for a mine shaft below.

That is, that a thing is man-made is not a token,
necessarily, of unnaturalness. Simply the black hole of loss,
sucking in light, lets out a sob—a spoken
word, the one that is said in drawing to a close.

What is said? What is said gets lost
in the noise of the air. What is said has to tell
that the earth is a pause, a repeated pause
like a double track: intermittent, parallel.

Fuga et vita

1

Ушло единственное, что было,—как кровь ушла,
как с языка слюна, или влага и соль из глаз,
как тень из комнаты в коридор—ни рубца, ни шва,
щелкнули клавишей на стене, и свет погас.

Только на то и хватает за жизнь ума,
чтобы понять, что она всегда позади.
Только жизни и есть, что она сама,
она и ее заклинание: не уходи.

Не потому так плохо, что то ушло,
в чем вся любовь была, все дыханье мое,
а потому, что было так оно хорошо,
что без него нет хорошего. Без нее.

2

Я был, лишь где ты была,
где звёзды как ни сложись,
вырезывает топор-пила
тебя по общим лекалам, жизнь,

где сплошь, как клейма, твои следы
на всем, на каждом шагу,
на каждом зерне, и звене воды
и крови, и на моем мозгу.

Я ничего не знаю кроме
тебя, но знаю, что что ни встреть
тобой не оттиснутое в уме,
то будешь не ты, а смерть:

пусть я наткнусь в ней на красоту—
тем горше: без красоты
той, где в благоуханном поту,
с кровью под кожей—ты.

Fuga et Vita

1

The only thing that was is gone, as blood is gone,
as spit gone from the tongue, from eyes the salty moisture dried,
a shade slipped from the room, no scar is left, no seam,
on the wall a switch clicked once, out went the light.

Only sufficient reason remains in life to grasp
that all of life is past, everything I know,
Only enough of life for life herself,
life and her refrain: don't go, don't go.

It's not so bad because the thing that's gone
was filled with all my love, my very air,
but because of how it was so good, so good,
that without it, nothing's good. Without her.

2

I was only there, where you were,
where however stars align,
the axe-saw carves you out
according to the general templates, life,

where like a special stamp your trace
is everywhere, at every step,
on every grain and cell of water
and blood, and in my brain.

There's nothing that I know
aside from you, but no matter what
I meet, if not engraved by you
in me, it won't be you, but death:

and even if I meet with beauty there—
the more the bitter: without that beauty
where there is, in fragrant sweat,
with blood beneath the skin—you.

Кратер

В декабре девяносто девятого
на краю белоснежного кратера
мы стояли. А кто это—мы?
А такие ребята из Питера,
двое-трое, ну максимум пятеро,
обступившие скважину мглы.

А вокруг из тумана и зелени
урожай новогоднего семени
колыхался, как воздух в жару,
и земля, как больная жемчужина,
вся в испарине мелкой, простужена,
бормотала одно: не умру.

Не умрем!—восклицали мы Северу
и стучали по голому дереву.
Не умрем, потому лишь, что—мы!
И клялись над отверстием в кратере,
как над люком ковчега на якоре
среди пены последней зимы.

Вздору было с добром—но и главного:
нимб святого на гравий для ангела
шел, чтоб вымостить тропку в саду
монастырском—где сплошь гладиолусы,
завиваясь, вплетались нам в волосы
в девяносто девятом году.

Горизонт расширялся поблизости
не к простору, однако, а к лысости,
отчего мы спадали с лица.
Но казалось: немного усилия,
и распустится кратер, как лилия,
и столетью не будет конца.

Crater

In December nineteen ninety-nine
we stood on the rim of a snow-white
crater. Who's the "we" in mind?
From Piter a bunch of guys
(two or three, maybe five)
surrounding a hole in the haze.

Out of the fog and greenery around us
the New Year seed harvest quivered
like air hot with a fever,
and the earth like a huge, ill pearl
all droplets of sweat, down with a cold,
muttered over and over, "I won't die."

"We won't die!" we cried out to the North
and knocked on the trunk of a tree.
We won't because we're we!
And swore it over the crater's mouth,
over the hold of an anchored ark
in the swirls of last winter's foam.

Sense and nonsense mixed, but what mattered
was the way a saintly halo laid out
a gravel path for an angel
through the monastery garden where
the gladioli in their windings twined
in our hair in nineteen ninety-nine.

The near horizon began to clear,
not wider and wider but smooth and sheer,
which made us feel sad again.
But it turned out, with a little effort,
the crater would open like a lily
and the century would never end.

Цирк

Через час представленье. В своей уборной гимнаст,
надевая трико, кружит голову ассистентке—
говорит очень громко, что храбр и на что горазд,
обращаясь к тонкой, их разделяющей стенке.

Одновременно выходят. Прогуливаются к зверям.
В загоне слабая видимость. Не вовсю, но воняет.
Что-то чавкает, дышит. Сниженный вариант
обстановки, которая всех к сближенью склоняет.

Ты погляди, говорит он, ты погляди на него:
этот царственный лев, его царственность бесподобна.
Царственность, рыкает лев, любезное вам фуфло,
съесть бы обоих—жаль, человечество несъедобно.

Все-таки прыгает на решетку. Чем не атлет!
Ассистентка уводит взгляд от его гениталий,
поворачивается к гимнасту, думает: чем не лев!
Волосы, прежде всего, и зовут Виталий.

Цирк!—приходит им в голову, —честное слово: цирк!
Лев вспоминает газель, правда, в качестве яства.
Ассистентка—другого гимнаста, но тот был псих.
Гимнаст—как он начинал без крюка и балласта.

Circus

The show starts in an hour. In his dressing-room as he pulls
on his tights, an acrobat makes his helper's head whirl
he talks so loudly, saying he's brave and bold as a bull,
his voice booming through the thin wall between him and the girl.

They come out simultaneously, saunter across
to the animals. There's a stench from the cages; things are lit dimly;
a heavy tread, heavy breathing: Call it a lower-case gloss
on the set-up that draws everyone into the family.

Take a look, he says, take a look at him:
That's the king of the cats, has a kingdom like no other.
For you, roars the lion, "king" is a typical spin;
I'd eat you both, but humans are inedible fodder.

All the same he leaps to the grille—an athlete, that!
She looks down at his penis below his great mane
and up at the acrobat, thinking: Just like the big cat!
full head of hair, to begin with, and Vitaly the name.

O the circus!—it hits them—it's really The Circus!
The lion remembers "gazelle"—true, as pungent food;
the girl, a previous actor—albeit one that was quirky;
and the acrobat—his first steps without balancing pole or hook.

Коршун

Коршуны плачут …
«Агамемнон»

Коршун—откуда он вынырнул, коршун,
нá гору ветра взобравшийся шерп!
Зренье—как крови неотпертой поршень,
крылья—как месяца черный ущерб.

Только как будто он в страхе сегодня,
в страхе, растерян, как ласточка хил,
всех отчужденней, всех тварей безродней,
всех обреченней. Что с ним, Эсхил?

Что-то же хочет он выразить, коршун,
визгом, холодным, как режущий серп,
незаглушаемым, жалобным, горшим
ужаса им облюбованных жертв.

Это вспоровший брюшинную полость
голос, но не предсказаний и притч,
а не-его, им не признанный голос—
к битве, заведомо гибельной, клич.

Он проиграл ее. Он умирает.
Пусть не сейчас—но уже предала
жизнь. И задел уже хвост его краем
всплывшие без левитаций тела.

Он не согласен, он борется. Коршун
он! И, не зная, как выместить зло,
что-то еще выясняет с сотворшим
волю, и небо, и клюв, и крыло.

94

The Black-Winged Kite

The kites are weeping …
                              —Agamemnon

A kite—where did it come from, the kite,
this Sherpa climbing a mountain of wind!
Its eye pounds like a piston of closed-circuit blood,
its wings are like the black wane of the moon.

Except that today it seems to be frightened,
to be frightened and lost, as frail as a butterfly,
cut off from everyone, least of all creatures,
doomed beyond others. Aeschylus, why?

Seems to want to communicate, the kite does,
with an ice-cold shriek that cuts like a scythe,
unsparing, plaintive, far more bitter
than the terrified cries of the victims it picked.

This is a voice tearing open the belly
but not telling the future or moral tales,
and not its, not its own voice really,
but a war-cry to battle sure to be fatal.

It lost it. Now it's dying. Even if
not at once, life has by now given way.
And the edge of its tail has already biffed
all the bodies that surface but don't levitate.

It doesn't accede, it fights back. It's a kite!
And not knowing how to take vengeance for spite
clears up something else with the creator
of will and sky and beak and wing.

—Вы одна, и я один. Нам бы … —Да пошел ты!
—Жаль. А то пучок нарвал я иван-да-марьи,
грубо-фиолетовый, примитивно-желтый—
лучших в нашем не нашел полу-полушарье.

От сплошной стены Кремля до сплошной Китая
луг да луг у нас, кой-где тронутый футболом,
почему и вся-то жизнь бледная такая
в два малярных колера с именем двуполым.

—Что вы хочете сказать?—Две-три вещи. То есть
что страна у нас—трава с огоньками станций,
что, вобще, родимый край—то, где ездит поезд,
и что есть еще балет, дед-и-баба-танцуй.

—Не болтайте языком. —Языком и вытру.
Да, картинка дешева—но ведь не дешевка,
в первом классе выбрал сам бедную палитру,
ржавый фиолет чернил и сиротский желтый.

Тем оно и бередит Лермонтову душу,
что былинкой восхищен и ничтожной тварью
на обломках корабля выплывший на сушу
и целует, не стыдясь слез, иван-да-марью.

* * *

"You're alone, and I'm alone. We ought—" "Oh, get lost!"
"That's a shame. Because, look, I've a bunch of Johnny-jump-ups here,
a crude kind of violet, primitively yellow,
couldn't find a better in our semi-hemisphere.

"From the Kremlin wall itself all the way to China
we have meadow after meadow, some soccer-made contextual,
but somehow all of life's a pallid underliner
in two selected art colors both called bisexual."

"What are you trying to say?" "Two or three things. I mean,
the country we have is green grass with stations' fiery flames,
and in general our native land is where they run the trains,
and besides, there's the ballet for the dancing old man and his dame."

"Stop wagging your tongue." "I'll wear my tongue out.
Sure, the painting's cheap but it's not cheap stuff,
in the first class I myself picked a poor palette out,
inked in rusty violet and a mild yellowish buff.

That's how it brings back the old Lermontov karma,
each blade of grass sends me, and through even the lowest scup
on the wreck of a ship that sailed onto terra firma,
not holding back its tears, it kisses the Johnny-jump-ups."

Настроения

Городское

Город, полис, мегаполис,
ненасытимого брюха
потный блеск, бессонный голос,
потаскуха, потаскуха,
золотых коронок город,
пломб цементных, черных дыр,
город-ястреб, город-голубь,
третий Рим и третий мир.

Потускнел в гербе твой ратник
от кромешных допечаток,
лаком ты покрыт, бомжатник,
можно трогать без перчаток,
так как племя полуголых
нимф и приодетых бонз
утолило первый голод
свой бомжом—а ими бомж.

Что глотали, чем кололись,
морок глаза, греза уха:
место зрелищ, шоу-полис,
показуха, показуха—
город-глюк. Но я прописан
здесь. И жил, И, тьфу-тьфу-тьфу,
выжил. Я им весь пронизан.
Он мой дом. Я здесь живу.

Moods

Urban

City, *polis*, megalopolis,
the vast insatiable belly's
sweaty sheen, sleepless voices,
strumpet, strumpet, nighttime nellies,
city of the golden crowns,
of concrete fillings, blackened holes,
falcon-city, pigeon-town,
Third Rome again, third world.

On the coat of arms your warrior's faded
from infernal extra printings;
you're lacquered over, homeless native,
touchable with gloveless fingers
because the tribe of semi-naked
nymphs and dandily dressed men
wiped out hunger with homelessness—
and the homeless tribe, with them.

What they swallowed stuck inside,
eyes confounded, ears filled with dark
dreams: shows, shows *polis*-wide,
amusement parks, amusement parks—
peace-pill city. But I'm registered here.
And I've lived here. And whatever you say
I've hung on. It goes all through me.
It's my home. Here I'll stay.

Дачное

Что блаженней, чем сквозь листья
небо видеть в гамаке
и искать систему в свисте
пароходов на реке

и, кукушками осмеян,
счет ведущими до двух,
всласть хореем, гибким змеем,
щекотать гортань и слух?

Что блаженней, чем для Дженни
или Мери или Сью
приводить размер в движенье,
флиртовать строкой вовсю,

погружаться в зной приязни,
вспоминать тропу к воде
и не знать, ты где—на Клязьме,
или Темзе, или где?—

всё (само собой) неспешно,
невсерьез, чуть-чуть, слегка,
по-английски, безмятежно,
не вставая с гамака.

Vacation Land

What's more blissful than from a hammock
to look at the sky through the leaves
and to try to figure out the pattern
of boat whistles on the river

and, teased lightly by the cuckoos,
counting regularly to two,
to your heart's content like a snake in chorus
tickle your throat and your ear, too?

What's more blissful than for *Jenny*
or for *Mary* or for *Sue*
to provide a model of something moving
by flirting flat out with a verse,

to let go of yourself in the heat of friendship,
to recall the path to the water's edge
not knowing where you are—on the Klyazma,
or the Thames, or where?—

everything (of course) moves slow,
is unimportant, is easy pieces,
is casual, like English, without
(from the hammock) your ever getting up.

Деревенское

За акацией, за ивой
в перестроенной избе
я живу один, счастливый,
не скучая по Москве.

Да и даль-то: сяду в «Ниву»,
двести верст прогрохочу—
вот он я. Но нет, не двину
рычагов—ну, не хочу.

А хочу пройтись до Волги,
попытать, хорош ли клев,
снять, вернувшись, Флакка с полки,
насушить боровиков,

и под Шубертовы песни …
Что?! А то, что стены крен
вдруг дают—и «ну как если!»
между слов звенит рефрен.

Ближних, дальних—нет усадеб.
Не дозваться. Страх перво-
наперво: «А ну как схватит!»—
я один, и никого.

Схватит душу, схватит горло,
схватит вся тоска и ночь,
и вся память, и вся прорва
боли, ужаса и проч.

И нагрянет, зубы скаля,
домовых и леших рать.
Страшно, Галя, страшно, Галя,
страшно, Галя, умирать.

Rural

Under an acacia, under a willow
in a simple, rebuilt peasant house
I live by myself, perfectly happy,
not missing Moscow evenings out.

As for distance: I climb in my *Niva*,
shake off two hundred versts of dust,
and there I am. No, I don't actually
touch the levers. Going's a bust.

The Volga is what I'd like to reach
to see if the fish are biting, and after,
once home, take Horace down off the shelf
and dry the boletus that I gathered,

and listening to some Schubert again—
what?! why, it's the walls are heeling
all of a sudden—and that "what if" feeling
jangles between the words in refrain.

Near or far—there's no other farm or center.
No one to answer when I phone.
Fear comes first: "That's all there is!"
There's nobody around; I'm alone.

The soul shuts down, the throat catches,
the nighttime longing closes in,
and what I remember and all the snatches
of pain and horror and other such things.

The army of demons of house and woods,
baring its teeth, draws suddenly nigh.
It's frightening, Galya, frightening, Galya,
frightening, Galya, to be starting to die.

Азбука

Где в слове дух? Где, то есть, ужас в *ужасе*?
А я скажу! Он в *эс* и *жэ* и *у*.
Их, этих трех, кто сколько бы ни тужился,
ужасней не найти. Я так скажу:

дух слова—буква. Сумма букв. Ни менее,
ни более. Покой и пропасть в *о*
не то что бездна *а*. Все дело в пении
по буквам, по крючкам—я вот за что!

За азбуку без слов! За просто азбуку
от *а-бэ-вэ-гэ-дэ* до *э-ю-я*.
Что значит—"кто заказывает музыку?"!
Здесь все, что есть, заказываю я.

От *а* до *я*. Я надуваю воздухом,
согретым кровью легочной, тельца
прозрачные; ввожу их в дрожь нервозную
голосовыми связками певца.

Да и немых их лент, кудряво-перистых,
довольно, чтоб в восторге, не дыша,
глядеть, как льнет *эл-эм-эн-о к пэ-эр-эс-тэ*,
е-жэ-зэ-и к у-эф-ха-цэ-че-ша.

104

An ABC

Where's a word's spirit? I mean, where's the fright in *frightened*?
I'll tell you! It's in the *f* and *r* and *i*.
I swear you'll never find a thing more frightening
than those three no matter how hard you try.

I'll say it out: the spirit is the letter.
The sum of letters. No more, no less. Peace
and precipice in *e* aren't bottom's *o*.
Singing letters, making hooks—so we please!

I'm for a wordless ABC! An ABC
from *a-b-c-d-e* to *x-y-z*.
What does it mean when people ask, "Who called for music?"
Here everything that is was called for by me.

From *a* to *z*. With air warmed by the blood
of my lungs I blow up transparent body cells;
I build them into a nervous system of tics
and tremors by a singer's vocal chords.

And enough of their dumb, curly-feathery chains
comes through so, breathlessly, you can see
with delight how *l-m-n-o* clings to *p-r-s-t*
and *e-f-g-h* holds on to *u-v-w-x-y-z*.

* * *

Наступает суббота—но сна ни в одном,
и бормочет слеза: для чего я ползу,
безразличная к выводу, жизнь ли вверх дном,
или просто нет сна ни в едином глазу.

Наступает суббота—а все, что вблизи,
расплылось, как в пару очертанье колес
паровоза, хоть ясно, что все на мази,
а слеза—от усталости век и желез.

И пора начинать—то ли день, то ли что,
только как, если не было сна ни в одном,
если время—что после субботы, что до,
ни труда, ни покоя ни ночью, ни днем.

* * *

Saturday's dawning—couldn't get to sleep,
and a teardrop is mumbling, "Why should I creep,
what's the difference whether life's not right,
or it was just a sleepless night."

Saturday's dawning—but everything near
is dissolved, like a steam-engine's wheel in the steam,
though it's clear things are going as smooth as a dream,
and fatigue in the eyelids and glands made the tear.

And it's time to get going—if day it will be,
only after a night of not sleeping—which way,
if time, post-Saturday, as well as pre-,
isn't work, or repose in the night, or the day.

* * *

… skip that lipstick …
Billie Holiday

Мотылька губной помады
на рубашке на плече
не прихлопывай, не надо,
не споласкивай в ручье.

А войди с ним, глаз не пряча,
в дверь, где прошлое прожил,
в обворованную дачу,
в развалившийся режим.

Встань под сводами пропорций
чистых—вспомни, однолюб,
как возвел ты и испортил
жизнь, не красившую губ.

И зрачком в зрачок подруги
немигающим упрись
так, чтоб медленные струи,
скорбь смывая, полились.

* * *

… skip that lipstick …
Billie Holiday

Don't brush away that butterfly
of lipstick on your shoulder-seam,
don't worry, don't you even try
to rinse it in the steady stream.

Bring it on in, don't hide your eyes,
come in to where you lived your past,
this vandalized, once cozy home
what's left of a regime's collapse.

Stand up beneath the clean design,
of arches that you built and tainted—
remember then, one-woman man,
a life whose lips were never painted.

Look deep into your girlfriend's eye,
unblinking, let your pupil stay
to let the slowly flowing streams
begin to wash the grief away.

* * *

Кто ночью уставился в звездное небо, тот жив.
Бесспорно. Не нужно, ни зеркальце чтоб запотело,
ни дрогнули веки—когда на кристальный массив
наглядно, как туча, находит галактики тело.

А все-таки знака бы! Кашля. Простой суеты.
Ответа, доносится Шуман с окна, или Шуберт.
И в небо глядим и в глядящего—я или ты.
Что, словом, и вправду из нас кто-то ночью не умер.

Нет времени спорить, что время не время, а путь
от точки до точки; от точки инстинкта, положим,
до точки восторга—когда убеждает не ртуть,
а оптика в том, что не космос безжизненный ожил.

* * *

Whoever has gazed at the night full of stars is alive.
Without doubt. No breath-fogged mirror is needed, no proof,
no flutter of eyelids—when, clearly, the galaxy's body
will lean like a stormcloud low down on a crystalline roof.

Still, some sign would be good. A cough. Some such trivial thing.
An answer to whether that's Schumann or Schubert outside,
from the window. That we look at the sky and the one who is looking—
you or me. That one of us really didn't die in the night.

There's no time to argue that time is not time, but a road
from one point to another. From an instinctive point, let us posit,
to the point of pure rapture—when optics, not mercury, show
that what came to life was no mere inanimate cosmos.

Двенадцатое июня

День двенадцатого июня, тихий, белый,
не предвещает ничего, чего не случилось
вчера и во все июни—кроме исторических, конечно,
из них единственного я был свидетелем 41-го.
Пасмурно, но не мрачно; не холодно, а прохладно;
наверное, будет дождик.

Двенадцатое, я вспомнил, лежа в постели
блаженнейшие четверть часа, когда и не спишь, и не действуеш
день Исаакия Далматского,
                        в который родился царь Петр Великий,
в честь чего и поставил Исаакиевский собор в Петербурге.
Я об этом услышал, когда был молод, от митрополита
                        Рижского Леонида.
Он прибавил: «А я ленинградец»—я поддакнул: «Я тоже».

Возможно, разницей со вчерашним
надо считать то, что мне предстоит побриться—
в деревне я бреюсь не каждое утро.
А так—все то же, помыться и причесаться
да проговорить «Помилуй» и «Благодарю, что
                        живой проснулся».
Даже в магазин не ездить—
вчера из села, где лавка, привез хлеб и сметану.
(И две бутылки водки и сигареты,
но это Тишке напротив, он, увидав, что еду, выскочил
                        из калитки—
и дурочке Ангелине: ждала, как всегда, на дороге.)
Так что крикнуть через забор Николавне,
                        чтоб редиски мне нарвала и укропу,
сварить овсянку, и день покатился.

Вчера было солнце и жарко, потом набежала гроза,
прогрохотала, обрушилась, и опять солнце.
К вечеру Тишка, веселый,
                        аккуратно складывал сброшенные с

June Twelfth

June twelfth—the day is calm, clear,
forecasting nothing that hasn't happened
yesterday and every June—except for historical events, of course,
one day of which I witnessed in '41:
overcast but not gloomy; not cold but chilly;
most likely, a shower coming.

The twelfth, I recalled, lying in bed
a blessed quarter of an hour when you're neither asleep nor awake,
was Isaac Dalmatsky's Day, the day on which Peter the Great was born,
in honor of which St. Isaac's Cathedral in Petersburg was built.
I had heard about that when I was young from Riga Metropolitan Leonid.
He added, "But I'm from Leningrad," which I seconded, "Me, too."

Perhaps the difference from what happened yesterday
lay in the fact that I still had to shave—
in the country I don't shave every morning.
Everything else is the same: wash, brush my hair,
and repeat "Have mercy on us" and "Thanks that I awoke alive."
No need to go shopping—yesterday I brought bread and sour cream
                    from over town, where the store is.
(And two bottles of vodka and cigarettes
but Tishka across the street, seeing me going, popped out from his gate,
and silly Angelina, she was waiting on the roadside, like always.)
So over the fence came a shout to Nikolavna to pick me some radishes
                    and dill,
cook up some porridge, and the day was under way.

Yesterday was sunny and warm, then a storm struck,
it thundered and lightninged, it poured, and the sun came out again.
Towards evening, Tishka, feeling cheerful, carefully stacked a pile of
                    boards he had tossed off his tractor
and chatted with Angelina, while she laughed like a wild woman.
He said, "You gave me the cold shoulder, Angelina," and she went
                    "Ha, ha, ha!"

трактора доски
и болтал с Ангелиной, а та по-звериному хохотала.
Он говорил: «Выставила ты меня, Ангелина»,—
                            а она: «Га-га-га»—как кикимора.
Оказалось, он ей налил сто грамм, упросила—
про свои поллитра при этом ни слова, приняла в одиночку.

На закате—а какой закат одиннадцатого июня? считай,
                            никакого—
шаталась она из конца в конец по деревне, шаталась
                            и вдруг давай орать песни
про кавалерийские ночи Спасска и Волочаевск
и про шаль с каймой, наброшенную на плечи.
На мотив неизвестный—но его соблюдала строго.
Наконец умолкла, только ходила и бормотала.
Николавна с крыльца окликнула: «Что, напелась?»
Она ответила: «Это горе мое напелось».

Да, такого сегодня, двенадцатого, уже не будет,
а что будет, узнаем тринадцатого, завтра.
Что из этого следует? Следует, как обычно,
что нет ни будущего, ни, увы, настоящего, одно прошлое.
Да уже и не прошлое, а неведомо что.
Что и было—а при этом и не было.

Прошлое—Исаакий, Петр, июнь 41-го,
митрополит, Ленинград, эскадроны Гражданской—
                            это до 18 лет, 22-х, ну 25-ти,
а потом—только собственное, где ты сам был.
Вот попил бы с Ангелиной, да с ней попел бы,
а прежде того с ней пожил бы и, главное, полюбил бы—
                            хоть ненадолго,
и, возможно, не свелось бы все целиком двенадцатое
к бритью трехлезвийным «жиллетом» и одеколону «кашерель»
после чего кожа такая свежая и чистая,
что ее все время хочется гладить.

like a female hobgoblin.
It turned out he had poured her a hundred grams, she talked him
into it—
about her own half liter at the same time not a word, drank it by herself.

At sunset—what kind of a sunset was there on the eleventh? Thinking
about it, none—
she went weaving from one end of the village to the other, weaving and
suddenly shouting songs
about cavalier nights in Spassk and Volochayevsk
and a specially trimmed shawl thrown over the shoulders.
Not clear what the tune was, but she stuck to it.
Finally she fell silent, just kept walking back and forth and mumbling.
From her porch Nikolavna called, "So, sang yourself out?"
She replied, "That was my grief singing itself out."

Indeed, today, the twelfth, won't be like that,
though what it will be like we'll find out tomorrow, the thirteenth.
What does that prove? Proves, like always,
that there's no future, nor—sorry to say—a present, only the past.
And that's not really a past but nobody knows what.
What actually was—and at the same time wasn't.

The past is Isaac, Piter, June '41,
the metropolitan, Leningrad, the Civil squadrons—up till 18, then 22,
maybe 25—
after that, only your own world, wherever you yourself were.
I mean, I might have had a drink with Angelina, and gone singing
with her,
or more likely than that lived with her some, or, chiefly, fallen in love
with her, though not for long,
and perhaps everything about the twelfth wouldn't have come down
to shaving with a triple-bladed Gillette followed by Cacherel aftershave,
which makes your skin feel so fresh and clean
that you want to pat it all the time.

* * *

Чем меньше остается знать,
тем глубже в узнаванье ярость
вонзает шпоры—тем загнать
необходимей насмерть старость.

Вихрь свежего песка в струю
часов, идущих без починки,
врываясь, сносит на краю
дыры висящие песчинки.

И в знанье—жалкое число
их, и во времени, но малость
обоих не внушает жалость:
их горсть, но в этой горсти всё.

* * *

The less there is remaining to be known
the deeper into recognition rage
digs in its spurs—the more hard-pressed
the drive toward death becomes for age.

A vortex of fresh sand abruptly swells
the hour-glass stream that flows beyond repair,
and sweeps away the grains from where they cling
above the hole, the last few hanging there.

Of what is known—a pitiful amount,
of time as well, but though the count is small,
no pity is required—it only makes
a handful, but a handful holding all.

Поминки по веку

Кто висел, как над трубами лагеря дым,
или падалью лег в многосуточных маршах,
или сгнил, задохнувшись на каторжных баржах,
обращается к молодым
через головы старших—
тоже что-то бубнящих, с сюсюком нажим
чередующих этаким быстрым, особым,
наглым, модным, глумливым, угодливым стебом,
что от воя казенного не отличим
над публичным пустым его гробом.

До свиданья, идея идеи идей.
Спи спокойно, искусство искусства, величье
пустоты, где со сцены ничтожным злодей
уходя, возвращается в знаках отличья
от людей. От людей.
Дух эпохи, счастливо. Знакомым привет.
Незнакомым—тем более: ходят в обнимку
те и эти, слыхать, соответствуя снимку,
хоть засвеченному, хоть которого нет,
но ведь был же—а что еще век, как не снимки?
Будь, фотограф. Будь, свет: ляг, где лег, холодей.
До свидания, сами поминки.

И до скорого, мать, и до встречи, отец.
С богом, мной обернувшееся зачатье
в спешке, в августе, в схватке без цели. И счастье
от ключами во мне закипавших телец,
мной клейменых … Пока, но отнюдь не прощайте.
Факт, увидимся. Здесь не конец.
Закругляйтесь. Кто хочет добавить,
то есть кто-то другой, не как я, не такой,
добавляй. А столетию—вечный покой.
Веку—вечная память.

A Wake for Our Time

He who has hung like smoke above labor camp stacks
or fallen like carrion on long forced marches,
or rotted, crushed to death in hard-labor barges,
turns to young flacks
over older heads, themselves
muttering, mumbling, their mouths thin cracks
alternately lisping in a rapid, odd,
impudent, modish, sardonic, obsequious pidgin
indistinguishable from official wailing
over his public, empty coffin.

Good-by, idea of idea's ideas.
Sleep tight, art's art, grandeur
of vastness, where a worthless villain leaves
the stage but to return with medals of merit
nobler than others. Nobler than others.
Spirit of the age, good luck! Friends, my best.
And especially to people I've never met:
See, some are strolling, arms round each other, like in a snapshot
well lit maybe—or maybe not
at all, though it existed, our time—for isn't a time the snapshots
                         it makes?
OK, photographer. OK, world: lie down where you lay, cool off.
Good-by yourself, wake.

So long, Mother. Father, till our next meeting.
Blessings on you, hasty conception that became me
one August in a mindless encounter. And on the cheering
from the homunculi bubbling up in me stamped
with my brand. See you later, but in no sense farewell.
This isn't the end. Fact: there'll be more greetings.
Round off to the nearest. Whoever wants to add lines—
I mean someone else, not someone like me,
go ahead. To the century I wish peace forever,
and "Eternal Rest" to our time.

Веку то, веку се, веку Богом отпущенный век—
и в архив! Как альбом, как досье, как кассету—на полку.
Потому что в раскопках искать его после—без толку:
он был цель, то есть будущее и разбег,
просто множил число человек
на число километров и ставил под оперный снег,
засыпающий действие, как новогоднюю елку.
Сам уют—симуляция ласк и индустрия нег—
для культуры не слой. Обернем мокрой тряпкой метелку
и протрем на прощанье светелку.
И загоним под плинтус просроченный чек
и иголку—
ту, которой нам Хронос навел на запястье наколку,
ставя нас на ночлег.

What with this and with that, our time's God-forsaken—
So, into the archives! Shelve it like an album, a dossier, a CD—
because trying to dig it up later is sheer stupidity:
Aimed at the future and all of its run-up,
it simply multiplied the number of people
by the kilometer numbers and set the result like a Christmas tree
under the opera snow that covered the act.
The shelter itself—a pretense of affection and a factory of leisure—
is no coating for culture. Let's wrap our broom in a rag
and wipe out the attic at parting.
And let's sweep under the skirt board the out-of-date check and
                              the needle
Father Time used to fasten our wrist with a bracelet
when he put us up for the night.

NOTES

Along an Ancient Thought-Tree
Title refers to lines from the *Tale of Igor's Campaign* about how thought is like a squirrel running along a branch. "rastekashesia mysliiu po drevu" can be read as "mys'iu," that is to say, squirrel. Hence the "wolverine." The *Tale*'s author later writes "skacha, slaviiu [solovei], po myslenu drevu" [jumping, as a nightingale, along an ancient thought-tree].

Ode on an Easel
"a monastery, turned museum"—the Cloisters (New York City).

Alone on a Hill
Alexander Ivanov (1806–1858) developed an intense interest in rendering landscapes and trees during his last years in Italy, before returning to Petersburg.

Kirillov: Character in Dostoevsky's *Demons* who had traveled to America.

A Little Song
Simone Martini: (circa 1280–1344), Italian painter, who was one of the most original and influential artists of the Sienese school. The reference is to Martini's *The Virgin of the Annunciation*.

Portrait of St. Petersburg after a Century
The city landscape described here is that of the area where Anna Akhmatova lived in the years after the Revolution of 1917.

On the Death of ***
"... Aeneas to a certain European man": Anna Akhmatova, in her poems addressed to Isaiah Berlin, juxtaposes the lyrical hero with Aeneas, who abandoned Dido.

Lullaby for Sophie
Vladimir Solov'yov (1853–1900) Russian poet and religious philosopher. At the center of his philosophy is the concept of Sophia, the Wisdom of God.

The Ballad of the Black Card
A pee-wee is poker slang for a low card.

Crater
Piter is a commonly used nickname for St. Petersburg.

"Don't brush away that butterfly ..."
The epigraph is from "Don't Explain," written by Billie Holiday
and Arthur Herzog, Jr., as sung by Holiday.

Other titles from the series

IN THE GRIP OF STRANGE THOUGHTS

A series of books featuring poets introduced in the bilingual anthology In the Grip of Strange Thoughts: Russian Poetry in a New Era, *which presents poetry at the critical turning point away from Soviet life to a reclamation and renewal of Russian culture and individual voices.*

Salute to Singing
Gennady Aygi
Translated by Peter France

These variations on folkloric themes are born out of the Chuvash and Turkic motifs that Aygi grew up with, and which Aygi and France have collected in their work on Chuvash poetry. Now in his 60s, Aygi continues to be celebrated as the Chuvash national poet, and as a major poet of the Russian language.

"Peter France's scrupulous versions are faithful not simply to the often ambiguous sense of the originals, but also to the typographical minutiae ... which spell out the exclamations, questionings, pauses, vulnerabilities and praises of this most remarkable poet."
—TIMES LITERARY SUPPLEMENT

Poetry / 96 pages
Paper (0-939010-69-0) $13.95

A Million Premonitions
Viktor Sosnora
Translated by Dinara Georgeoliani and Mark Halperin

Reaching back into medieval Rus' and forward into metrical and linguistic innovation, Sosnora has written with a wide-ranging and unique voice. Historical allusion, conscious anachronism, humor, and intensity of word-play dominate by turns his continually protean poetry.

Poetry / 144 pages
Paper (0-939010-76-3) $12.95

The Score of the Game
Tatiana Shcherbina
Translated by J Kates

Shcherbina emerged in the early 1980s as a spokesperson for the new, independent Moscow culture. Her poetry is now widely published in both established and experimental journals at home and abroad, and has been translated into Dutch, German, French, and English. Shcherbina's poetry blends the personal with the political, and the source for her material is pulled from classical literature, as well as French and German cultural influences.

Poetry / 128 pages
Paper (0-939010-73-9) $12.95

A Kindred Orphanhood
Sergey Gandlevsky
Translated by Philip Metres

An integral member of the Seventies Generation, Gandlevsky was one of the underground Russian poets who wrote only for themselves and their circle of friends during the Brezhnev era. Despite their relative cultural obscurity—or perhaps, precisely because of their situation as internal émigrés—the Seventies Generation forged new directions in Russian poetry, unfettered by the pressures that burdened Russian writers both before and during the Soviet period.

"Out of the Rubik's Cube of Russia rise the complex strains of Sergey Gandlevsky … superb translations that uncannily make the Russian ours." —ANDREI CODRESCU

Poetry / 136 pages
Paper (0-939010-75-5) $12.95